11. 00

The Collected Poems of
Earle Birney

The Collected Poems of
Earle Birney

Volume II

McClelland and Stewart Limited

The Canadian Publishers
McClelland and Stewart Limited
25 Hollinger Road, Toronto

Printed and bound in Canada

CONTENTS/II

1955-1962: México

1958-1972: Asia

1959-1965: Canada

1962: South America & the Caribbean

The Poems

1955-1962: Mexico

SIX-SIDED SQUARE: ACTOPAN

Do tell me what the ordinary Mex
Madam, there is a plaza in Actopan
where ladies very usual beside most rigid hexagrams
of chili peppers squat this moment
and in Ottomíac gutturals not in Spanish lexicons
gossip while they scratch there in the open

    But arent there towns in Mexico more av—? Dear Madam,
    Actopan is a town more average than mean.
    You may approach it on a sound macadam,
    yet prone upon the plaza's cobbles will be seen
    a brace of ancients, since no edict has forbad them,
    under separate sarapes in a common mescal dream—

        But someone has to work to make a—Lady,
        those ladies work at selling hexametric chili,
        and all their husbands, where the zocalo is shady,
        routinely spin in silent willynilly
        lariats from cactus muscles; as they braid they
        hear their normal sons in crimson shorts go shrilly

bouncing an oval basketball about the square—
You mean that all the younger gener—?
I mean this is a saint's day, nothing rare,
a median saint, a medium celebration,
while pigeon-walking down the plaza stair
on tiny heels, from hexahemeric concentration

within the pyramidal church some architect
of Cortés built to tame her antecedents—
You mean that Mexico forgets her histor—? Madam, I suspect
that patterns more complex must have precedence:
she yearns to croon in Harlem dialect
while still her priest to Xipe prays for intercedence.

Actopans all are rounded with the ordinary
and sexed
much as they feel. *You mean—*
they are more hex-
agon and more extraordinary
than even you, dear lady, or than Egypt's queens.

1955

FRANCISCO TRESGUERRAS*

Half out of your coffin,
Francisco Tresguerras,
you cast a wry look at us,
asking the way.

To the right and the left of you,
off to their Heaven,
their Hell, they go clambering,
all your squat townsmen,
certain of Something,
ignoring your question.
Only you are left clueless,
no man for a queue.

Down here their descendants
avoid still your eye;
black mists of old women
and huddled rancheros
point the nose to the pavement
while round them your columns
rise slender and soaring
into reaches of grace
and trumpets of light.

They have hung up once more
all the clutter you banished;
misshappen pieties
pockmark the sheerness;
mock-blood of a god
drips from your dome.

Yet out of your fresco,
down on the lot of us,
Francisco Tresguerras,
still stares out your face
holding question and answer.
Your Heaven, your Hell is
half out of your coffin
still to be asking,
still the creator,
while the centuries move,
right left and right left,
from the vision arrested,
from the Limbo of art.

Celaya 1955

*Born Celaya, México, 1759; died there, 1833. Self-taught architect, sculptor, engraver, poet; introduced neo-classical form into the churches of his town, in opposition to the elaborate rococo style prevailing before (and after). One of his churches preserves his *Last Judgement*, containing a self-portrait.

IRAPUATO

For reasons any
                brigadier
                            could tell
this is a favourite
                nook
                            for massacre
Toltex by Mixtex Mixtex by Aztex
Aztex by Spanishtex Spanishtex by Mexitex
by Mexitex   by Mexitex   by Texaco

So any farmer can see how the strawberries
are the biggest
                and reddest
                            in the whole damn continent
but why
                when arranged
                            under the market flies
do they look like small clotting hearts?

1955

LATE AFTERNOON IN MANZANILLO

Señores Lukas and Faustino
            medicos from Tulancingo
in the surge
            beyond the leafgreen harbour
play seriously with surfboards
Their pregnant wives in the *cabaña*
            toy with rums

Back in the steaming port
            is Jesusito

hammering
        with somewhat malarial languor
a shrimpboat
        to the ribshapes
            of the galleons
Cortés launched toward the Philippines

In the membraned mud below the scaffold
his daughter Tita
        scabbed and naked
            as a beanpod
kneels rocking her small dead fish
        to sleep
in a decaying turtle shell

El Capitán Jasón Castillo y Mordita
shoulders his golden braiding
        through the shitten air
rolls in a fugue of sporting
        up the Street of Games
crossing the already
        strabismic
            eyes
of the chess-carver tiptapping
        in his brick cave
and swings at the Lane of Roses
where sits among others
        the slightly older
sister of Tita
        by a hitching post
on the wildwest verandah

Maria turns the dominoes and
        rhythmic
            prays
that the Dark Virgin
        with her hand
            will cool
this new pain
        surging in her crotch

Colima 1955

PACHUCAN MINERS

All day in a night of lurch   blast
bend   they have deepened the dark search
their precortesian priests began
into the cold peak's argent
mysteries   Only the ore has risen
into the tasselled wind and run
on singing rails beneath the ardent
sky to sorceries beyond their vision
But now another nugget sun
himself is floated out of thought
and   Orphic and helmeted as divers
are pressed upwards all the miners

Under thin stars by murky troughs
white-eyed they spit   wash rockscurf off
turn without rancour from the guarded gate
below the white Olympus of the gringos
Helmed still and wordless they tramp down
base-metalled roadways to the town
stop where peons by their braziers
shiver to sell them roasted maize
Yet like a defeated army still
descend past blackened walls above
the tree-abandoned valley till
at the lowest street the doors of light

peal out   tequila is a brightness
in the throat   bottles and faces gleam
receive them in a sensible dream
In the cantinas helmets roll
backs fling upright   O now legs are male
are braced   each knotty pair   to hold
up song and hurl it at the night
then step their own way down to where

deep in her torchy den
snakes Toltecan looping in her ears
her crucifix agleam above the sheet
Eurydice reclines and hears
the wild guitars   and daily waits
the nightly rescue of her silver men.

México 1955

PROSPERITY IN POZA RICA

With a gnarled stick
in a gnarled hand
the Indian ploughed
the ashen land

With the derrick's fist
through the blackened soil
the Mexican plumbs
to lakes of oil

In the honking town
the lawyers treat
the drillers drink
and the beggars eat

On the slithering hills
in hands of brick
the Indian ploughs
with a gnarled stick

State of Vera Cruz 1955

STATE OF SONORA

Thin country with the bright hard
hide   Rain ricochets from adamantine
ranges where wild peccaries
scrabble   and clatters
intact down baked
ravines with morning shard
of culverts and swart hill-pine
back to the sea   By noon sun cakes
and over the river's bones
trucks flash and rattle
under a glassy sky   Life crusts
a shell
on the surface or   like scales   flakes
Around the prickly
pear to the tarmac
boys   like chestnuts   naked skip
or stricken
wither to death across adobe sills

By puma-coloured crossroads
with names dry and implacable
as locusts—
Chirriones   Bacarac
Los Muertos—
men pad weeklong after lean
sheep and flinteyed goats through cracks
of thin dust between
the joints of cactus-
armoured land

Then in a Sunday of brassbands   peyote
and firecrackers
dance on slaphappy *huaraches*
through cobbled plazas
till they drop down
drunk to sleep on the radiant highway
with scrannel chickens and the bony cows

Or in stone towns that plead
with the sun for softness—
Hermosillo   La Palma   El Oasis—
under the small beauties of peppertrees
the leathered rancheros chew sinewy steaks
and spit pomegranate seeds
at the lustrous flies

At dusk off Guaymas   where sharp-
winged and zinc-white the pelicans
skim to the quick blaze of marlin
leaping from sapphire swells
the fishermen turn backs gnarled
as turtles on the day sizzling
into the Sea of Cortés
and point home for the lights diamonding
in chalky huts on the timeless
cliffs   their stark boats slapping
over the flattening rollers that smack
and are bounced back
by the guano-glazed islands

México 1956

SINALÓA

Si señor, is halligators here, your guidebook say it,
si, jaguar in the montañas, maybe helephants, quién sabe?
You like, dose palmas in the sunset? Certamente very nice,
it happen each night in the guia tourista
But who de hell eat jaguar, halligator, you heat em?
Mira my fren, wat dis town need is muy big breakwater—
     I like take hax to dem jeezly palmas.

So you want buy machete? Por favor I give you
sousand machetes you give me one grand bulldozer, hey?
Wat dis country is lack, señor, is real good goosin,
is need pinehapple shove hup her bottom
(sure, sure, is bella all dose water-ayacints)
is need drains for sugarcane in dem pitoresco swamps—
    and shoot all dem anarquista egrets.

Hokay, you like bugambilla, ow you say, flower-hung cliffs?
Is ow old, de Fort? Is Colhuan, muy viejo, before Moses, no?
Is for you, señor, take em away, send us helevator for w'eat.
It like me to see all dem fine boxcar stuff full rice,
sugar, flax, rollin down to dose palmstudded ports
were Cortés and all dat crap (you heat history?)—
    and bugger de pink flamingos.

Amigo, we make you present all dem two-wheel hoxcart,
you send em Québec, were my brudder was learn to be padre—
we take ditchdiggers, tractors, Massey-Arris yes?
Sinalóa want ten sousand mile irrigation canals,
absolutamente. Is fun all dat organ-cactus fence?
Is for de birds, señor; is more better barbwire, verdad?—
    and chingar dose cute little burros.

Sin argumento, my fren, is a beautiful music,
all dem birds. Pero, wy you no like to ear combos,
refrigerator trucks? Is wonderful on straight new ighway,
jampack wit melons, peppers, bananas, tomatoes, si, si. . . .
Chirrimoyas? Mangos? You like! Is for Indios, solamente,
is bruise, no can ship, is no bueno, believe me, señor—
    and defecar on dose goddam guidebook.

Mazatlán, México 1956

20

NAYARÍT

From   moonwastes of lava

brighT ^t_t air $^twi^st_s$ $d_{o_{wn}}$ $_a$ $m_{i_{l_e}}$ of

                                  b
                                  a
                                  r
                                  r
$^s_{l}$ivering on ^th_e ^wa_y t_{h_e} $^{u}_{q}i^{te}_{e^s}$$_{t}{^h}$$_a^t$ ^n_c_a
                                 M

S ^{pR} $_{aW}{^{ls}}$ to s^{o}lve the eq=ations of

buried
$_p{^{yr}}{^{am}}id_s{^{id}}_s$ and $^s_{l}$$i{^{n}}k_s$ $^d_e{w}$ HEa $^a_n{_d}$
                           Vy

dULLing   over the le a ky $p^a{^{lme}}$$^t{_t}_o$
                                  roofs

Only $a^{roun}d$ the asTOUNdinG ochre/and/ash
                         l
white of the a/esuohoohcsyra
                b   o   r
              so ute yc nempo
               l l   t

and the bLACk CE of the coffeewarehouse
                  UB
                       t y r o t c a
and the   (blank)
                       o b a c c o f
                ^{T}
is the air brigh^T_T again and haRRRD

                     t
and l u U U n a ^{t}t_{tt} T ttttttttt *tic*

Tepic, Mexico 1956

AJIJÍC, LAKE CHAPALA

This hip gringo can't wait to tell you
the place rhymes with tee-HEE   He'll
have another *tequila*
make it añejo
muchas gracias
Rolling the Spanish is nothing to him
for as the morning sun
quickens the sapgreen swords
of the banana trees and the shimmer
of flies in the patio
so do his goofballs
brighten his liver

From under the bar he lugs out
his six feet of representational nonart
already sold
to the *patron*
who has a heart of sorts
& his brushes
camera
IOUS
There is moreover something
not quite affection
between him and the madrona-brown Mixtecan
boy who serves him now with careful
noisiness

At sundown will arrive the *mariaches*
The starchy guitarist will cast
his one good eye's black glitter
on this *norteamericano*'s
by-then-bloodshot face

Outside
the fishermen will pass
and the blobs of *pescada blanca* in the nets
rubbing over their shoulders
will flake their bare shanks with mica
as they trudge
(Lawrence must have watched their fathers)
from the still retreating
but as yet Mexican
lake

Guadalajara 1956

HOT SPRINGS

Here's a hotel where even the stairs
cascade with elixir
Moctezuma washed in these springs
    and not just to keep clean   *no señor*
    it was recommended for gout
    it was in the days of Diaz
    when *caballeros* had gout

Now
        IT REMEDIES
      THE CONSEQUENCES
      OF BUSINESS STRAIN

or to put it straight on the line

IT ACTIVATES THE GLANDULAR SEXUAL SYSTEM
      BOTH MALE AND FEMALE

wheeeee!
Here come the blacksuited old bankers
plump small generals
retired   except from their uniforms
even   watch the step *señor*
a leading firecracker millionaire

And FEMALE?
These downycheeked *chiquitas*
sliding their little pomegranate bottoms
out from the Italian sports cars
surely have come only to render
supplementary thermal assistance

By the cantina across from the carpark
the dusty goatherds are sipping *pulque*
in the open while   with their fiery old eyes
they casually shoot every general
and strip the laughing ladies

Nueve Ixtapan 1956/1962

SESTINA FOR THE LADIES OF TEHUÁNTEPEC

"*Teh*. has six claims to fame: its numerous hotsprings
(*radioactive, therapeutic*); moderate earthquakes
(*none in several years*); herbivorous iguanas
(*eaten stewed*); Dictator Porfirio Diaz
(*d. 1911*); its hundred-mile-wide isthmus;
and the commanding beauty of its Indian women."

Stately still and tall as gilliflowers the women
though they no longer glide unwary past the hotsprings
naked as sunlight to each slender softer isthmus
now that ogling busloads (*Greyhound*) make their earth quake
And still skirt-bright before the flaking palace of old Diaz
(*hotel*) they gravely offer up their cold iguanas

Their furtive men (*unfamed*)   who snare iguanas
sliding on tree-limbs olive-smooth as are their women's
have fallen out of peonage to landlord Diaz
into an air more active than their tepid hotsprings
more prompt with tremors than the obsolete earthquakes
rumbling through their intercontinental isthmus

From the stone music of their past the only isthmus
from astronomic shrines fantastic as iguanas
to this unlikely world (*3 bil.*) that waits its earthquake
is their long matriarchal ritual of women
whose eyes from fires more stubborn than under hotsprings
flash out a thousand Mayan years before a Diaz

Goldnecklaced   turbaned   swaying in the square of Diaz
volute and secret as the orchids in their isthmus
braids black and luminous as obsidian by hotsprings
beneath their crowns of fruit   and crested live iguanas
rhythmic and Zapotecan-proud the classic women
dance (*v. marimbas*) their ancient therapy for earthquakes

O dance   and hurl flamboya   till the cobbled earth quakes
let your strong teeth shine out in the plaza lost to Diaz
toss your soaring sunflower plumes   sunflowering women!
Hold for all men yet your supple blossoming isthmus
lest we be noosed   consumed with all iguanas
and leave the radiant leaping of the lonely hotsprings

Beneath all hotsprings lie the triggered earthquakes
Within this gray iguana coils another Diaz
Is there a green isthmus walking yet in women?

Salina Cruz, México 1956

CONDUCTED RITUAL:
SAN JUAN DE ULÚA

Wholehearted natives used this isle
for carving out the cores of virgins.
Cortés, more histrionic, purified it
with a fort and modernized the Indians
in dungeons contrived to flood each time
the tide was high. Later the pirates,
internationally impartial, fired it,
baking both sides, and later yet
the Mexicans and gringos had a turn
(killed by Yanqui shells in eighteen-forty-seven:
soldiers ninety, civilians two-eleven).

And still it lies an isle of sacrifice.
Eyes conquistadorial and burning
above their Aztec noses, acolytes
with skullandcrossbone armbands from
the Oficina de Tourista
suffer the willing files to come
before the neverfailing mysteries,
and hold the virgin hearts aloft
where bled to death lies history.

Veracruz 1956

GUADELUPE

Ah señoritas
with permanent seats
in the bullring
and escorts who know headwaiters
in Paris
it's not till you park
your Alfa Romeos
a quartermile from the shrine and
coifed in black lace from Aragon
crawl on your silken penitential knees
over the cobbles
that I see you have Mexican blood
running with sins and anesthesias
richer than any my veins will ever carry

México City 1956

BELDAMS OF TEPOZTLÁN

These osprey-beaked
and plucked old birds
bring values to linguisticism
To hawk
a fake idol
to a Kansan down in Cuernavaca
they wheeze an English
For the citizens a purring Spanish
will unload a lottery ticket
But back and perched beside the village well
they'll need four octaves at least
of Aztec clicks
to verbalize a decent quarrel

México 1962

MEMORY NO SERVANT

but a stubborn master

Eight years ago weekend in Veracruz
It was sugary hot no doubt
I'm sure my bed was a hammock
cocooned in cheesecloth

Oleander? There must have been . . .
past the fountains down to the sea
which I rather think was too warm
. . . or were they hibiscus?
Somebody else recalls that the meals
were good and cheap
I have some colour slides that surprise me
with improbable cascades
of bougainvillea between gold-cups

But what I can be sure not to forget:
  Ten feet from the first bridge
  on the highway north from the town
  a turtle coming up from the Gulf
  Both right wheels ran over its middle
  The sound a crushed carton
  Looking back—
  the untouched head
  ancient stretched and still
  moving

México 1956/Ithaca 1963

1958-1972: Asia

TWO TRANSLATIONS FROM MAO TSE-TUNG

1. MIDSTREAM*

Alone in a cold autumn I stood
Where Hsiang-chiang flows north
Past the point of Orange-Grove Isle.
The ten thousand hills were crimson,
In crimson tiers the forest.

Up the great hyaline river
Struggled a hundred vessels.
Eagles in the vast air poised to strike;
Fish in the shallows hovered.
Each living form under the frosty heaven
Fought with another for freedom.
I stared from a desolate tower
And asked the immense earth—
Who decrees the rise, the fall?

With a hundred friends now, returning
I range back over the rainbow days,
The crowded risky years.
O schoolmates, in youth blossoming and tall with talents,
We must now in the arrogance of our knowledge
Uproot our scented careers.
Fingering mountains only, and rivers,
To hold poetry alive in our minds,
We will use for manure
Those bygone dreams of ten-thousand-household fiefdoms.
Don't you remember, once it has reached midstream
Your craft shoots over
As the rapids take flight?

*To "translate" Chinese poems without having any knowledge of Chinese, even when aided, as I have been, by a Chinese scholar with a rich historical and aesthetic understanding of the poems, is to stand on a remote hill looking wistfully toward a complex and fascinating landscape which cannot even be entered. My "interpretation", even if successful, can only be a sketch of some of the obvious visual outlines of the poem's world. To supplement it, I add three "versions" of the first poem's five opening lines, in which, with the help of Professor Ho, I have tried to glimpse other features of this world from other lookout points on my still alien hilltop.

Version I is the bare literal translation supplied me by Professor Ho. It gives no indication, however, of the maze of secondary meanings, historical glancings and other subtle overtones of which Professor Ho is conscious and of which I can become aware only after much glossing and explication by him.

Version II consists of a transliteration by Professor Ho, together with his speech accents as they sound to my ear. Their effect strikes me as being much closer to Old English than to modern English poetry and I have accordingly utilized the Anglo-Saxon devices of primary (/), secondary (\), and light (◡) stresses. The reader should be warned, however, that Mao Tse-tung's poem is written to a known classical tune, and its accentuation, when so rendered, is quite different, and subordinated to a complex tonal pattern quite untranslatable.

Version III is my attempt, on the basis of Versions I & II, to arrange English words in an approximation to the rhyme-effects, speech-accents and basic meaning of the same five lines. The result can be of value only to illustrate the impossibility of approaching, in modern English, the concentration of Chinese poetic style.

These versions are preceded by my free renderings of this poem and of "Snow", in which I have attempted to produce readable English poems with as little deviation as possible from the sense and spirit of the original.

Version I

> Alone stood, chilly autumn,
> Hsiang-chiang flows north,
> Orange Isle at tip.
> Beheld ten-thousand hills all red,
> Layers of forest all tinted. . . .

Version II

> Tŭ-li hán-ch'iu.
> Hsiáng-chiang péi-chŭ.
> Chŭ-tzŭ chóu-t'óu.
> K'ắn wắn-shăn hứng-pièn.
> Ts'eng-lín chín-jaǹ. . . .

Version III

> Alône stóod I—
> Hsiang-chiang nórth glides—
> Sáw pàst Orange Ìsle
> All hillsides léaf-reddenĕd,
> Trée-tiers crímsoned. . . .

U.B.C. 1957

2. SNOWSCAPE FROM A PLANE

How northern clean is this vision!
Below, a thousand miles are sealed with ice,
ten thousand around us are whirling with snow.
Look, from the Long Wall's either flank
only a vast wildering stretches now;
up the Great River's length and down,
all the mighty tumbling is mute.
Silver serpents are dancing on the mountains,
wax elephants prance over the high plains,
and we would measure our own soaring with the skyloft.
If we could wait for all clouds to clear,
perceive the red earth-maiden in white furs,
what strange beauties would bewitch us.
Seductive ever are mountains and rivers,
luring even the heroes of history to fall at their feet.

A pity that the original Imperator of Ch'in
and the Martial Emperor of Han
disclosed only very modest literary abilities,
that the high founders of T'ang and Sung
ranked somewhat low in versification,
and even he who was Heaven's proud son throughout a generation,
Jenghiz Khan,
could bend his bow only to bring down a gyrfalcon.
These have all gone.
But in assessing the glamorous ones
wait—let us see who rises this morning.

WIND-CHIMES IN
A TEMPLE RUIN

This is the moment
   for two glass leaves
dangling dumb
   from the temple eaves
This is the instant
   when the sly air breathes
and the tremblers touch
   where no man sees
Who is the moving
   or moved is no matter
but the birth of the possible
   song in the rafter
that dies as the wind goes
   nudging other
broken eaves
   for waiting lovers

Nara, Japan 1958

A WALK IN KYOTO

all week   the maid tells me   bowing
her doll's body at my mat   is Boys Day
also please Mans Day   and gravely
bends deeper   the magnolia sprig in my alcove
is it male   the old discretions of Zen
were not shaped for my phallic western eye
there is so much discretion
in this small bowed body of an empire
(the wild hair of waterfalls combed straight
in the ricefields   the inn-maid retreating
with the face of a shut flower)   i stand hunched
and clueless   like a castaway in the shoals of my room

when i slide my parchment door to stalk awkward
through lilliput gardens framed & untouchable
as watercolours   to streets looking much as everywhere
men are pulled past on the strings
of their engines   the legs of Boys
are revolved by a thousand pedals
& all the faces are taut & unfestive as Moscow's
or Toronto's   or mine

Lord Buddha help us all there is vigour enough
in these islands & in all islands reefed & resounding
with cities   but the pitch is high   high as the ping
of cicadas (those small strained motors concealed
in the propped pines by the dying river) & only male
as the stretched falsetto of actors mincing the roles
of kabuki women   or female only as the lost heroes
womanized in the Ladies Opera—
where in these alleys jammed with competing waves
of signs in two tongues & three scripts
can the simple song of a man be heard?

by the shoguns palace   the Important Cultural Property
stripped for tiptoeing schoolgirls   i stare
at the staring penned carp that flail
on each others backs to the shrunk pools edge
for the crumb this non-fish tossed
is this the Days one parable
or under that peeling pagoda the 500 tons
of hermaphrodite Word?

at the inn i prepare to surrender again
my defeated shoes to the bending maid   but suddenly
the closed lotus opens to a smile & she points
to where   over my shoulder   above the sagging tiles
tall in the bare sky & huge as Gulliver
a carp is rising   golden & fighting
thrusting its paper body up from the fist
of a small boy on an empty roof   higher
& higher   into the endless winds of the world

1958

BANGKOK BOY

On the hot
cobbles hoppity
he makes a jig up
this moppet
come alive from chocolate
sudden
with all
small
boys'
joy
dancing under the sun
        that dances
        over the toy king's
        claw roofed palace
        and blazes the roof
        above the latest Hong Kong girlies
        imported to strip
        to the beat of copulation
        and shimmers the broken-china towers
        where ten thousand Buddhas
        sit forever
        on other boys' ashes
In his own time
naked
laughing he
on the scene's edge
like a small monkey-
man
in the endless Ramayana fresco
skips
        that frozen fresco
        of old wars
        under still another glittering Wat

where tourists worship
in a regalia
of cameras
pacing out their grave
measures
along the enormous stone-still
god
or splaying
to immortalize
the splayed gyrations
of temple dancers
Beat out
brown smallfry
beat out your own
wild
jive
under this towering strayed
tourist and his bright
strange
cold—whee!—
coin in your small paws
before in his own motions
he vanishes
in the fearful tempo of a taxi
to that spireless palace
where god-tall
in their chalked goblin-faces
all tourists return
to plod in pairs like water-buffalo
by a bare hotel pool
to their funeral music
Prance
this dazzled instant
of your father's big
Buddha smile
and all the high
world bang in tune
the bright

sun caught
cool
        before in the high world's
        clumpings
        you are caught
        slid lethewards
        on choleric canals
        to where the poles of klongs
        and rows of paddyfields
        are shaped to bend
        small leaping backs
        and the flat bellies
        of impets
        are rounded with beriberi
Scamper little Thai
hot on these hot stones
scat
leap
this is forever O for
all gods' sakes
beat out
that first
last
cry of joy
under the sun!

1958

THE BEAR ON THE DELHI ROAD

Unreal   tall as a myth
by the road the Himalayan bear
is beating the brilliant air
with his crooked arms
About him two men   bare
spindly as locusts   leap

One pulls on a ring
in the great soft nose   His mate
flicks   flicks with a stick
up at the rolling eyes

They have not led him here
down from the fabulous hills
to this bald alien plain
and the clamorous world   to kill
but simply to teach him to dance

They are peaceful both   these spare
men of Kashmir   and the bear
alive is their living   too
If   far on the Delhi way
around him galvanic they dance
it is merely to wear   wear
from his shaggy body the tranced
wish forever to stay
only an ambling bear
four-footed in berries

It is no more joyous for them
in this hot dust to prance
out of reach of the praying claws
sharpened to paw for ants
in the shadows of deodars
It is not easy to free
myth from reality
or rear this fellow up
to lurch   lurch with them
in the tranced dancing of men

Srinagar 1958/Île des Porquerolles 1959

1959-1965: Canada

SUNDAY NIGHTFALL IN WINNIPEG

& dust blowing round the Emperor
of India George v by the Grace of God
& the C.P.R.

cafe empty except for a waitress
who wont answer an honest hello
& cant serve beer

back into Portage Avenue
the filth of the week attacks
in a whirl from the gutter

other old loners
one with a nose like a rotting peach
is arguing passionately
with himself

on the corner a drunk lowers
his white pow
to belch at a pair of women in levis:
    fi bucks fer one of *yer* dirty twats!
    woodn give yuh a fart furrit
    yuh fuckin nitchies!

wind blows but the stink hangs
along this deadtreetrunk of a city

globefaced matrons shine
from a photographer's window
& there's a dim blowup
of Portage Avenue in 1901
—the same façades looking clean
& the street a river of space
without cars

on the gritted pane suddenly
i see behind me the faraway Sun
driving a last shaft
between deepblue rainclouds

i walk alone in the wind & the dusk
toward the beautiful
antediluvian
sky

Manitoba 1959/1970

FIRST TREE FOR FROST

When I was five   before the freeze went deep
my father dug me from the bush a sleeping
spruce   all greenness and limp claws
We planted it beside the gate to grow
with me   Her crown was just below my nose

But all she did that endless winter was
to make herself a cave of snow   and doze
When ground came back I topped her by my lips
In June she seemed to waken at the tips
Just keep it watered   even spruce must drink
my father said   Right through the summer's heat

I lugged jam-bucketsfull and watched my giving sink
down to those feet I could not see
That water was so cold it curled my hands
I felt the needles chilling on my tree
I stole hot kettle water   suds from pans
but those stiff branches never stirred for me
No prayers or heavings   nothing could begin
for all my care   to lift her past my chin

Then the white frosts crept back   I took
to slipping out when no one looked
and poured the steaming crescent of my pee
over the shivering body of my tree
That brown offering seemed to satisfy—
a warm tan mounted to her head

My father never understood   no more than I
why one day suddenly we found it dead
I've let trees go their own way since
Some things my loving never has convinced

Idaho State University 1960

HAIKU FOR A YOUNG WAITRESS

With dusk I am caught

peering over the holly

hedge at the dogwood

West Point Grey 1960

VILLANELLE

What shall I do with all my sea
your sun and moon have set alight
till you will swim along with me?

Its day, that lives outlandish free,
the flakes that fall within its night—
what will I do with all my sea?

How long on earth a refugee,
how far from water take the flight
till you have willed to swim with me?

Your room walls off transplendency.
These shores, the rising rocks, are bright—
what may I do with all my sea?

The strong day crumbles on the quay,
the windrows waste across the bight
till you will swim along with me.

I dive alone and grope to see
what salt and tidal things we might
but cannot reach with all our sea
till you have willed to swim with me.

Bowen Island 1961

SIXTH GRADE BIOLOGY QUIZ
(answers supplied by a rat)

To what order do the rats belong?
    To a superior order.
Where do they make their homes?
    In shelters underground
    below your lethal border.
How are their children born?
    From hydrocarbon links like yours
    but harder.
What do they eat?
    Your world's unguarded larder.
Why are they dangerous to human health?
    Because your health is our chief danger.
Have they any use for science?
    Yes, we trust in science, rodent science.
    Beneath your lab, your launching pad, your manger
    we carry on our underground research
    and learn more ways to multiply and wait
    till men have cleared themselves
    and cats
    and left the streets to glare at sky
    and there is freedom to preside
    for rats

Lieben 1961

NOVEMBER WALK NEAR FALSE CREEK MOUTH

I

The time is the last of warmth
and the fading of brightness
   before the final flash and the night

I walk as the earth turns
from its burning father
here on this lowest edge of mortal city
where windows flare on faded flats
and the barren end of the ancient English
   who tippled mead in Alfred's hall
   and took tiffin in lost Lahore
drink now their fouroclock chainstore tea
sighing like old pines as the wind turns

The beat is the small   slap   slapping
of the tide sloping   slipping
its long soft fingers into the tense
joints of the trapped seawall

More ones than twos on the beaches today
strolling   or stranded as nations
woolly mermaids   dazed on beachlogs
a kept dog   sniffing   leading his woman
Seldom the lovers   seldom as reason
They will twine indoors from now to May
or ever to never   except the lovers
of what is not city   the refugees
   from the slow volcano
   the cratered rumbling   sirening vents
   the ashen air   the barren spilling
   compulsive rearing of glassy cliff
   from city
they come to the last innocent warmth
and the fading
before the unimaginable brightness

II

The theme lies in the layers
made and unmade by the nudging   lurching
spiralling down from nothing

down through the common explosion of time
through the chaos of suns
to the high seas of the spinning air
where the shelves form   and re-form down
through cirrus to clouds on cracking peaks
to the terraced woods and the shapeless town
and its dying shapers

The act is the sliding out
to the shifting rotting
folds of the sands that lip
slipping to reefs and sinking cliffs
that ladder down to the ocean's abyss
and farther down through a thousand seas
of the mantling rock
to the dense unbeating black unapproachable
heart of this world

Lanknosed lady sits on a seawall
not alone   she sits with an older book
Who is it?   Shakespeare   Sophocles   Simenon?
They are tranced as sinners unafraid
in the common gaze to pursue
under hard covers their private quaint barren
affair   though today there is no unbusy body
but me to throw them a public look

not this wrinkled triad of tourists
strayed off the trail from the rank zoo
peering away from irrelevant sea
seeking a starred sign for the bus-stop
They dangle plastic totems   a kewpie
a Hong Kong puzzle for somebody's child
who waits to be worshipped
back on the prairie farm

No nor the two manlings
all muscles and snorkels and need to shout
with Canadian voices   Nipponese bodies
racing each other into the chilling waters
last maybe of whatever summer's swimmers

Nor for certain the gamey old gaffer
asleep on the bench like a local Buddha
above them   buttonedup mackinaw
Sally Ann trousers   writing in stillness
his own last book   under the squashed
cock of his hat   with a bawdy plot
she never will follow

A tremor only of all his dream
runs like fear from under the hat
through the burned face to twitch
one broken boot   at the other end
of the bench as I pass

dreaming my own unraveled plots
between eating water and eaten shore
   in this hour of the tired and homing
   retired   dissolving
   in the days of the separate wait
   for the mass dying

and I   having clambered down to the last
shelf of the gasping world of lungs
do not know why I too wait   and stare
before descending the final step
into the clouds of the sea

III

The beat beating   is the soft cheek
nudging of the sly   shoving   almost
immortal ocean at work
on the earth's liquidation

Outward the sun   explodes light
like a mild rehearsal of light to come
over the vitreous waters
At this edge of the blast
a young girl sits on a granite bench
so still as if already only
silhouette burned in the stone

Two women pass in a cloud of words
     . . . so I said   You're *not*!?
     and she said   I *am*!
     I'm one of the Lockeys!
     Not the Lockeys of *Out*garden surely
     I said   *Yes* she said   but I live
     in Winnipeg now   Why for heaven's *sake*
     I said   then you *must* know Carl *Thors*on?
     Carl? she said   he's my cousin by marriage
     He *is* I said   why he's *mine* too! So. . . .

Born from the glare come the freakish forms
of tugs   all bows and swollen funnels
straining to harbour in False Creek
and blindly followed by mute scows
     with islets of gravel to thicken the city
     and square bowls of saffron sawdust
     the ground meal of the manstruck forest
or towing shining grids of the trees stricken

At the edge of knowledge the *Prince Apollo*
    (or is it the *Princess Helen?*)
floats in a paperblue fusion of air
gulf   Mykenean islands
and crawls with its freight of flesh
toward the glare and the night waiting
behind the hidden Gate of the Lions

IV

The beat is the slap slip   nudging
as the ledges are made   unmade
by the lurching swaying of all the world
that lies under the spinning air

from the dead centre and the fiery circles
up through the ooze to black liquidities
up to the vast moats
where the doomed whales are swimming
by the weedy walls of sunless Carcassonnes
rising   rising   to the great eels waiting
in salt embrasures   and swirling up
to the twilit roofs that floor the Gulf
up to the crab-scratched sands
of the dappled Banks

into the sunblazed living mud
and the radiant mussels
that armour the rocks

    and I on the path at the high-tide edge
    wandering under the leafless maples
    between the lost salt home
    and the asphalt ledge where carhorns call
    call in the clotting air by a shore
    where shamans never again will sound
    with moon-snail conch the ritual plea
    to brother salmon or vanished seal
    and none ever heard
    the horn of Triton or merman

V

The beat is the bob   dip   dipping
in the small waves   of the ducks shoring
and the shored rocks that seem to move
from turning earth or breathing ocean
in the dazzling slant of the cooling sun

Through piled backyards of the sculptor sea
I climb   over discarded hemlock saurians
   Medusae cedar-stumps   muscled horsemen
   Tartars or Crees   sandsunk forever
and past the raw sawed butt
   telltale with brands
of a buccaneered boom-log
   whisked away to a no-question mill

all the swashing topmost reach of the sea
   that is also the deepest
   reach of wrens   the vanishing squirrel
   and the spilling city
the stinking ledge disputed by barnacles
waiting for tiderise to kick in their food
contested by jittery sandfleas
and hovering gulls that are half-sounds only
traced overhead   lone as my half-thoughts
   wheeling too with persistence of hunger
   or floating on scraps of flotsam

VI

Slowly   scarcely sensed   the beat
has been quickening now as the air
from the whitened peaks is falling
faraway sliding   pouring down
through the higher canyons and over
knolls and roofs to a oneway urgent
procession of rhythms

blowing the haze from False Creek's girders
where now I walk as the waves stream
from my feet to the bay to the far shore
where they lap like dreams that never reach

The tree-barbed tip of Point Grey's lance
has failed again to impale the gone sun
Clouds and islands float together
out from the darkening bandsaw of suburbs
and burn like sodium over the sunset waters

Something   is it only the wind?
above a jungle of harbour masts
is playing paperchase with the persons
of starlings   They sift and fall
stall and soar   turning
    as I too turn   with the need to feel
    once more the yielding of moist sand
    and thread the rocks back to the seawall

shadowed and empty now
of booklost ladies or flickering wrens
and beyond to the Boats for Hire
where a thin old Swede clings in his chair
like hope to the last light

eyeing bluely the girls with rackets
padding back from belated tennis
while herring gulls make civic statues
of three posts on the pier
and all his child-bright boats
heave unwanted to winter sleep

    Further the shore dips   and the sea   sullen
    with sludge from floors of barges   spits
    arrogantly over the Harbour Board's wall
    and only the brutish prow of something
    a troller perhaps   lies longdrowned
    on an Ararat of broken clamshells
    and the flakings of dead crabs

The shore snouts up again
spilling beachlogs glossy and dry
as sloughed snakeskins
but with sodden immovable hearts
heigh ho the logs that no one wants
and the men that sit on the logs
that no one wants
while the sea repeats what it said
to the first unthinking frogs
and the green wounds of the granite stones

By cold depths and by cliffs
whose shine will pass any moment now
the shore puts an end to my ledge
and I climb past the dried shell
of the children's pool   waiting like faith
for summer   to where the last leaves
of the shore's alders   glistening with salt
have turned the ragged lawns
to a battlefield bright with their bodies

VII

For the time is after the scarring of maples
torn by the fall's first fury of air
on the nearest shelf above brine and sand
where the world of the dry troubling begins

the first days of the vitreous fusing
of deserts   the proud irradiations of air
in the years when men rise
and fall   from the moon's ledge

while the moon sends   as before
the waters swirling up and back
from the bay's world
to this darkening bitten shore

I turn to the terraced road
the cold steps to the bland new block
the human-encrusted reefs
that rise here higher than firs or singing
up to aseptic penthouse hillforts
to antennae above the crosses
pylons marching over the peaks
of mountains without Olympus

Higher than clouds and strata of jetstreams
the air-roads wait the two-way traffic
And beyond?   The desert planets
What else?   a galaxy-full perhaps
of suns and penthouses waiting

But still on the highest shelf of ever
washed by the curve of timeless returnings
lies the unreached unreachable nothing
whose winds wash down to the human shores
and slip   shoving

into each thought nudging my footsteps now
as I turn to my brief night's ledge

in the last of warmth
and the fading of brightness
on the sliding edge of the beating sea

Vancouver 1961 /Ametlla, Spain 1963

FIGURE SKATER

Vancouver 1962/1970

```
┌─────────────────────────────────┐
│ ARRIVALS        Wolfville       │
│ Locals                          │
│ From Halifax     30 Mins L      │
└─────────────────────────────────┘
```

It was the hand that caught in me

Sudden as a beast the blizzard
had whirled on us   was gone
as quick over the hill and howling
through the next village   whose spire
could be glimpsed blotting out now
in a gray fury

And we are wading   a straggle of passengers
in town shoes   through a snowscape
clean and cosy as any Christmas card
the small firs like spunwhite candy
spaced on the ice-cream hillocks

Already the sunlight smoulders down
burning on the narrow tracks at the crossing
and fires the sleet that sheathes one flank
and the bland diesel-face of our train
so small and innocent now it has stopped

You wouldn't think from that little jolt we got!
. . . Speedin . . . Naw, in that storm he jes couldn see

   Green as a great bruise
   where the smooth flesh of the drifts
   has been savaged   the auto lies
   crumpled and akimbo
   like a beetle battered by catspaw

Flung it fifty feet . . . Yeah an him further . . .
This year's chevvy . . . Well we stopped fast enough

We stand   the unsilent   stamping
staring   to reduce to livable size
what is casually spreadeagled here in the snow

Should be a law about level cross—
Sure but we oughta wistled wen—Hell we did!
. . . Anybody know who he is?

   We too anonymous   one to the other
   but our breaths write on the air
   the kinship of being alive
   surrounding the perfect stranger

Christ it's too cold I'm gittin back . . .
Yep ain't nothin we kin do . . . Hey look
he's only gone three hunderd . . .

A thin man unprompted is gathering papers
slewed from a briefcase over the raddled banks
He slaps them free of flakes
and packs them carefully back in the case
Now he teeters   not knowing what to do with it
The brakeman plods up with a plaid blanket

Train gonna be held up till police come?
. . . No I'm stayin
Conductor was up to that farm phonin em

   The man with the case silently lays it
   next to the open palm
   the blanket has failed to cover
   He offers his only remark

Assizes is on up to Wolfville
Them's law papers

   The halfburied engine continues to tick
   with cooling   something live under the snow
   Each time we are startled

Lawyer eh? . . . Musta stalled on the track
grabbed his case got half out his door . . .
Yep nearly made it . . . Young feller too

    The sun has given way again to a black sky
    Most have tramped back to the train
    The rest of us circle about
    as if for somewhere to put down the guilt

Yer all lucky we dint go offa the tracks
. . . He's right   Can't blame the crew none

    Diesel shrieks and we jump
    The brakeman gestures   Turning at once
    we leave him beating his arms for warmth
    turn in a pleasure of hurry   to hop
    like schoolboys back in the steps we made
    eager for heat and motion   arrivals
    and shaping already what happened

    The train moves to its goal
    and scatters us from the scene forever
    The manner of hills   words   faces
    slides from the gloss protecting each mind
    We will forget even that scotched face perhaps
    waiting till the gay rug came down
    in a Christmas world

    But not surely the longfingered hand
    stretched in some arresting habit of eloquence
    to the last irrational judgement
    roaring in from the storm

    Or is it only in me that the hand hooked
    and I who must manage it now like a third?

Nova Scotia 1962

CREELEY

"there is an insistent tremble
from the night's drinking"
   not that
      but this
         not *a*
            but *the*
               way
                  to read
with the night's tremble
the way
   to make
      the poem
         the scene
            the baby
everything gentle
   even wistful
especially the lock
   of hair
      that claws
         for attention
and must be sadly
   trembly
      beautifully
         pushed
            away

Vancouver 1962

CAN. HIST.

Once upon a colony
there was a land that was
almost a real
country called Canada

But people began to
feel
different
and no longer *Acadien*
or French
and rational
but *Canadien*
and *Mensch*
and passional

Also no longer English
but Canadi*an*
and national
(though some were less specific-
ally Canadian
Pacific)

After that it was fashionable
for a time to be Internationable

But now we are all quite
grown up & fir-
mly agreed to assert our right
not to be Amer-
icans   perhaps
though on the other hand
not ever to be
unamerican

(except for the French
who still want to be *Mensch*)

New Orleans 1962

TESTIMONY OF A CANADIAN EDUCATIONAL LEADER

Sixty years it took to make me.
   Church taught me first: all men are sinners,
and Women Eves; yet God invites
     a few of us to His own private dinners.
To lower the odds, eleven to one, against
     the role of Judas, I prayed
with youthful resonance among the elders,
     seeing apostles were not born but made,
nor profits either, priests nor pundits.
     Perceiving too that he who starts like Saul
gets to the top, I led the brethren
     inventing pasts to turn us into Pauls.

Setbacks came. The built-in bulb
     I'd thought to use for sole illumination
began to spotlight beasts so foul they crazed me,
     convinced me I'd been saved for lone damnation.
With care some wits returned: religion
     and literature, I twigged, were synonyms,
and pleasant living can be made by showing
     how very much the better poems are like hymns.

Yet when the Thirties arrived (with mine) the Devil
     still would trip me. Highly I thought,
and for a brief time spoke, of Hitler. Certain
     uncertain ladies' flesh in vain I sought.
Was I too timid? or was it youthful Adam
     that I craved? I tried, and failed, to bed
my best friend's wife, and found the only climax
     came while slipping lies into her boyish head.

But God at last was kind to his awakened.
  The Forties brought me peace to watch a war.
Some rivals lost their lives, and all lost time.
  I was the humanism they were fighting for,
rose to be Head, ate better and wrote sonnets,
  assembled witty lectures from the scholars,
delivered them with pentateuchal fire,
  let others wed, or publish, banked my dollars.

Peace was touch and go. The veterans massed,
  staffs swelled, rebelled, committees multiplied,
and factions too. I wooed the strong above me;
  below I pushed them to the losing side.
I penned some Presidential speeches, helped
  three influential easterners to our D. Litts,
slid into boys' clubs, finance committees, churches—
  but still my enemies would not call quits.
Then just as my Satanic colleagues had it fixed
  with the Admin. to cast me out from here—
my God is good!—the Prexy's plane went down,
  and I was quickest to the New Man's ear.

A Dean has duties too, but also Deanlets.
  One weekend I was Acting President.
And were another plane to crash, and certain things
  told certain Regents—no, I'd not be hesitant.
I have learned all things requisite for rule:
  in academics women do not matter;
men, from the pinkcheeked freshmen up, are still
  the seed of Adam; be wariest when they flatter;
equally be prompt to offer every Donor,
  Regent's wife and Cabinet Minister, all laud;
make daily friends but keep none . . . And so I'll sup—
  Satan, take that long spoon away!—with God.

Herne Hill, London 1963

ON READING *THE MALAHAT REVIEW*

there is a skeleton
in victoria's cubburd
his name is robbing
robbing bluebreast
he has a complicated warple
it is an extra-territorial sound
full of *Boys' Own Annual* chortles
and Iowa cheerleader screams
he pushes a very elegant handcart
but it is only chestnuts he sells

1964

OIL REFINERY

Under the fume   of the first dragons
those spellbinders who guard   goldhoards under barrows
whole fields of warriors   wilted: even Beowulf
fell in balebreath   from firedrake fangs

Yet this hugest of Worms   though he outburst heaving
from deepest of meres   under farthest moor
is led leaping and leaping   at last to these shores
and hour by hour   overhewn and whelmed

Not without fury resists   flames in the night
blasts the world air   wans all blue day
Ho! a handful of thanes   in helmets threaten him
in silver keeps stab him   the old swartshiner
with gauges bedevil   with dials with cyclonesnuffers
endless they slaughter   that slimiest of Nadders

Hwaet! he is quick again   thousand-toothed Queller
whirls his ghost in our wheels   unleashes or locks them
Yea he twins twentyfold   twines in our graveloot
breath of that sly snake   stifles and clings
slides from our long ships   coils round our steadings
Eala! we are lost   in the spell of his loopings.

Port Moody, B.C. 1964

THE MAMMOTH CORRIDORS

> *From Vancouver, Canada's Pacific metropolis, the*
> *tourist may drive east over the smooth Trans-Canada*
> *Hiway through a*

Turning from the great islands drowning
in the morning's waves from Asia
my car heads me from the city's April
   cherry petals on the slick streets
   against the flayed mountains the billboards
   conjuring perfection   Tahiti
   orgasms of power   death insurance

> *thousand miles of towering Rockies to the prairies.*
> *Crossing from the north shore at the spectacular*
> *Lion's Gate, the motorist begins to trace in reverse*

Over the taut bridge   through the lonely park
my wheels will themselves to the shrieking

the spectacular route taken by the first explorers
and hardy traders. Stanley Park, with its convenient
thruway, aquarium, totem poles (exact replicas of
originals now stored for preservation) . . . a thousand
acres of playground where Indians once camped . . .

Around the highrisers   the sullen leisured
dogs   and the rolling realtors
Then the spastic traffic
of buyers and bought   pedlars of weed and soap
of acid and snow   of work and wonder
'as the world asketh'   in Skidroad's lanes

Blessed with relaxing airs, Canada's third
largest city offers . . . yacht basins, beaches,
. . . panoramic view, where a modest cairn com-
memorates . . . British navy in 1729 . . . possession
of the North Pacific coast from the Spaniards
who first came to trade with the natives . . .

Eastward an hour and the master I own
has rushed me to winter and wildness
and merely the gray road coiling and diminishing
upward like a dragon's tail swinges me off
from the unsupportable Real
    the tortured peaks
    only a breath more broken
    the blind dive of the canyons
    a scratch of a century deeper
    since those first compulsive whites
    the Searchers
    for gold   absolution   furs   Asia
    for a name   death   or mere difference
    came hurtling in improbable canoes
    heavy with liquor and fear
    bearing their beads and syphilis
    muzzleloaders and god

According to recent scientific theories, this
was the route taken by the earliest Indians,
at the end of the last Ice Age.

but from the truths that compel me
up the land's one nerve like a virus
to undo in a single day my father's lifetime
of westering
from my own lusts and neckties and novels
from ulcers   vitamins   bulletins   *accidia*
i lie unshielded under each motel's roof

Convenient to transcontinental railroads and a
four-lane hiway . . . offers American visitors every
modern . . . angler's paradise   big game . . .

under the uncontrollable cliffs and the starlight
falling on the same ice-bitten ranges
the first men saw

Having crossed from Asia to Alaska, and followed
the mammoths down corridors in the melting ice-cap,
these earliest Canadians are thought to have reached
a dead-end in their progress south, and been forced
to turn west from the Albertan plains into the Rockies
and so eventually came to the Pacific.

in that century the Siberians took   or more
(and took a hundred centuries ago)
to move by floes and hunger past the point
of no return   trailing the great woolly ones
    watching for the gleam of nine-foot tusks
    tracking   floundering in the newborn earth
    wolving by the black rivers that rattled
    from the glare of the narrowing icewalls
till the last red fountains
(*Mammuthus parelephas columbi*   his blood)
gushed on the boggy tundra
at the blind corridor's end

In the nearby museum, mounted specimens of
the wild life,

Surviving westward then over howling summits
the Siberians possessed these still fresh-hewn alps
(which i inheriting do not possess)
    They moved by day through bear and elk
    and by their killing
outliving sleep by capturing the deer's Wit
the Power of cougar
    in nets of dance and word
    the medicine of mask
    the threat of drum

and a spacious diorama outlining the story of
man. No charge.

Three mornings now from the applefoam
and the seas my Engine unreels me
out from the last gouged hills
like a bull straightens
into the prairie's arena
charges in a dazzle of snow the human mesh

Through Calgary, where the Blackfoot trail
once crossed, a four-lane artery helps speed
the traffic of Canada's greatest car-per-capita
city . . . in Bowness Park, life-sized models of
dinosaurs that once roamed the area

where all began for me
though the log cabin where first i was forced
into air
is a lost ghost under a vanished bridge
by a dying river

In 1912 Stampede Day was inaugurated to perpetuate
the finest traditions of the pioneer and cowpuncher . . .
now a week of parades, racing, rodeos, and other

An ash of ice whines at the cross of streets
A morning drunk is spattering curses
over a halfbreed girl in a blotched doorway

> *picturesque events . . . for the traveller from*
> *the west, Calgary is the beginning of the*
> *great Canadian prairie, which though largely*
> *treeless, contains some of the world's richest*
> *wheat-farms and oil deposits . . .*

Far and far to the east again
i am pulled to a sky of land
flattened white to the Pole
i am drawn against the unstillable winds
   the breath of that madcap virgin
   mother of ice
   who embraced it all
   a wink ago in the world's eye
   till the sun won us again
   with his roving glance
   and sent her shrinking and weeping
   frozen lakes over the upstart grass

> *To the north, however, the rich postglacial*
> *soil eventually gives place to tundra, perma-*
> *frost and Arctic conditions . . .*

Hoarding her cold passion she lies
the Greenland lodger
and the land's long face   and mine
cannot forget   is graved
with her monstrous rutting
Her time is our secret clock
She waits for all to slow
Then to lust back
wider than Europe and Pacific deep
   bringing her love   the rounded silence
     a long hard peace

1965/1972

1962: South America & the Caribbean

BARRANQUILLA BRIDGE

From its upstream coping
dark boys in breechclouts
fish for fruit
with buckets twisted from chickenwire
to let water through

Every few minutes a glistening orange
a grapefruit   even a papaya
may roll from a crowded stall
on the riverside market
float down to their low arch

Mostly what the children pull up
is fruit thrown away
because holed or wormy   rotten   pithy
But you can't tell good from bad
when they're swirling in muddy waters
whoever you are
till you've rescued them all

With falsetto curses
the small Colombians fling back the culls
to drift under the dark bridge
suddenly flash golden again
popping out on the downside
and triggering shrieks
from smaller quite naked boys
who also are fishing
Poised to catch anything that bobs
they hope always for the edible
perhaps a mango the big guys fumbled
firm   ripe   even saleable

So far today there's no pile of these
only a heap of watersoft frauds
But they're not just chucked away
As I watch   one of the brown smallfry
nips round the upstream bushes
softly shoves a bucketfull of discards
back in the oily current
to be hailed   snared   and rejected
all over again
by the big boys in breechclouts
It's the sort of rough justice
the weak can perform on powers above
(passers of counterfeit would agree
—and in Barranquilla   hunger
fortifies Gresham's Law)

1962

CARTAGENA DE INDIAS, 1962
Ciudad triste, ayer reina de la mar (Heredia)

Each face its own phantom
its own formula of breed and shade
but all the eyes accuse me back and say

    There are only two races here:
    we human citizens
    who are poor but have things to sell
    and you   from outer space
    unseasonable   our one tourist
    but plainly able to buy

This arthritic street
where Drake's men and Cole's ran
swung cutlasses   where wine and sweet blood
snaked in the cobble's joints
    leaps now in a sennet of taxi horns
    to betray my invasion
All watch my first retreat
to barbizans patched from Morgan's grapeshot
and they rush me
    three desperate tarantula youths
waving Old Golds unexcised

By an altar blackened
where the Indian silver was scratched away
in sanctuary leaning   on lush cool marble
    I am hemmed by a conga drum-man in jeans
    He bares a brace of Swiss watches
    whispers in husky Texan

Where gems and indigo were sorted
    in shouting arcades
    I am deftly shortchanged
and slink to the trees that lean
and flower tall in the Plaza
    nine shoeboys wham their boxes
    slap at my newshined feet

Only in the Indio market
mazed on the sodden quais
I am granted uneasy truce
Around the ritual braidings of hair
the magical arrangements of fish
the piled rainbows of rotting fruit
I cast a shadow of silence
    blue-dreaded eyes
    corpse face
    hidalgo clothes
    tall one   tall as a demon
    pass O pass us quickly

Behind me the bright blaze of patois
   leaps again

I step to the beautiful slave-built bridge
and a mestiza girl
   levels Christ's hands at me
   under a dangling goiter

Past the glazed-eyed screamers of *dulces*
swing to a pink lane
where a poxed and slit-eyed savage
   pouts an obscenity
   offering a sister
   as he would spit me
   a dart from a blowpipe

Somewhere there must be another bridge
from my stupid wish
to their human acceptance
but what can I offer—
my tongue half-locked in the cell
of its language—other than pesos
   to these old crones of thirty
   whose young sink in pellagra
   as I clump unmaimed
   in the bright shoes
   that keep me from hookworm
   lockjaw and snakebite

It's written in the cut of my glasses
I've a hotelroom all to myself
with a fan   and a box of Vitamin C
It can be measured
in my unnatural stride
that my life expectation
is more than forty
especially now that I'm close to sixty

older than ever bankrupt Bolívar was
who sits now in a frozen prance
high over the coconut trays
quivering on the heads
　　of three gaunt mulatto ladies
　　circling in a pavane of commerce
　　down upon spotlit me

Out of the heaving womb of independence
Bolívar rode　　　and over the bloody afterbirth
into coffee and standard oil
　　from inquisitional baroque
　　to armed forces corbusier

　　He alone has nothing more
　　to sell me

I come routed now　　　scuffling
through dust in a nameless square
treeless burning deserted
come lost and guiltily wakeful
in the hour of siesta
　　at last to a message

　　to a pair of shoes
　　in a circle of baked mud
　　worn　　　out of shape　　　one on its side
For a second I am shaken by panic
heat?humidity? something has got me
　　the shoes are concrete
　　and ten feet long

　　the sight of a plaque calms
　　without telling me much

En homenaje de la memoria de
  LUIS LOPEZ
  se erigió este monumento
  a los zapatos viejos
el día 10 de febrero de 1957

Luis Lopez? Monument to his old shoes?
What??? There was nothing else
and the square was asleep

Back through the huckster streets
the sad taxi men still begging with horns
to the one bookstore

  Si señor   Luis Lopez el poeta
  Here is his book
  Unamuno praised it   *si si*
  You have seen *los zapatos*?   Ah?
  But they are us, *señor*
  It was about us he wrote
  about Cartagena where he was born
  and died   See here this sonnet
  always he said hard things about us
  Said we were lazy except to make noise
  and we only shout to get money
  ugly too, backward . . . why not?
  it is for a poet to say these things
  Also he said *plena*—how say it?—
  plena de rancio desaliño
Full of rancid disarray!
  Si, Si, but look at the end, when old
  he come to say one nice thing
  only one ever about us
  He say we inspire that love a man has
  for his old shoes—*entonces*
  we give him a monument to the shoes

I bought the book   walked back
sat on the curb happier than Wordsworth
gazing away at his daffodils

Discarded queen   I thought   I love you too
Full of rancid disarray
city like any city
full of the stench of human indignity
and disarray of the human proportion
full of the noisy always poor
and the precocious dying
stinking with fear   the stale of ignorance
I love you first for giving birth
to Luis Lopez   suffering him
honouring him at last
in the grand laconic manner
he taught you

—and him I envy
I who am seldom read by my townsmen

Descendants of pirates   grandees
galleyslaves and cannibals
I love the whole starved cheating
poetry-reading lot of you   most of all
for throwing me the shoes of deadman Luis
to walk me back into your brotherhood

Colombia 1962/Greece 1963

ON CARTAGENA DE INDIAS, HIS NATIVE CITY
(Freely translated from the Colombian poet Luis Lopez, 1879-1950)

It's easy, weaving your alleys
—my fortressed home, ancestral hideout—
to dream up cross and cutlass, the sallies
with fuming torches . . . But that's all died out.
The caravels long ago floated away
with the ballads, the ladies' masks.
They're gone forever from your stagnant bay.
Oil isn't shipped any more in leather flasks.

In the high Spanish days some of your men were bold.
Tough as condors they shone tall in the day.
You weren't then a mere roost for the ringdove.
. . . . Still, full of your own familiar rancid disarray
you manage to win, even from me, that love
a man finds he has for his shoes when they're old.

1962

MACHU PICCHU

Stubbornness   when I practise it
looks to be no more operative on history
than Boadicea's   The Romans always win

So the lords of the Inca   grilling
in Cuzco on the spit of Pizarro
rather than say which mountain
hid the Holy City   seemed
for the next four centuries
to be as ineffectual as early Britons
      or late Canadians

73

The Virgins of the Sun
and whatever strong town
at last embraced them
vanished out of belief

Till another bullhead   gentleman geologist
a believer in myth
slashed his way straight up
in jungle tangled like monstrous mane
through ignorance and *fers de lance*
to bare these bones

        Crawling over them yesterday
        to peer with cold bellies
        down all three cliffs falling still
        through a mile of air and lianas
        to the snaking Urubamba
        there were four of us
                coffee planter from Surinam
                womanizing Rhodesian pitboss
                American missionary-doctor
                baldheaded professor (Canada)

Linking roofless palace   shop
and the precisioned cyclopean stone
of hut   temple   storehouse   tower
there are 3000 hand-hewn steps

        the doctor was short of breath
        the professor's feet were flat
        There was a vicuña
        near the lone châlet
        which the planter and the miner
        tried to corner and photograph
        It spat

Only the heavybladed grass
on the great terraces rising to the clouds
maintains the will of the makers

the grass and the dumb llamas that crop it
like beasts from another planet

What human leavings there were
necklaces   the bones of old women
and children   are gone down to museums
Did the men all leave for the war
Pizarro already had won?
And the handmaidens of the Sun?
On three sides the cliffs
continue to fall to the Urubamba

    Yesterday there were only four voices
    drifting over the gray courts   debating
       the speeds of various colour films
       the length a vicuña spits
       the statistics of malnutrition
       and the figures of girls in Lima

Considering how long Bingham searched
and how many lords died over flame
the words of four such acolytes
scarcely declare a cultural dividend

    But the truth is our talk was mainly
    to hide how we felt growing suddenly
    bodily back into the legend
    no conquistador hooked even
    his mailed finger into

Imagine the Spaniards finding this!
They'd have tumbled its devil's work
down all three canyons in a granite cloud
For it was too high and too far here
under the equatorial snows   to pervert
this miraculous exactitude of Incan stone
into basements for still another
San Juan de Something of peasant styes
supporting a surplus of uglified churches
in Christ's makeshift Peru

Today in fact   stirred
by quite nameless excitement
we have waked in the last dark hour
groped up stairs grooved and gouged
in the living rock   to stand
higher than the highest watchtower
like Brocken spectres magnified
on the black peak   and see the Sun
rise still on what was built
to worship Him

Brain and blood gone forever
skulldented   trepanned
but in all the dark sockets
of her fountains   on the broken rounds
of her streets   over the white fields
of play   her Sun glints and blesses
Picked clean of writhing vine or man
Machu Picchu eyes the swords of the Andes

while down the hanging terraces
four tourists descend
limping   puffing   longing
for meat   sleep   rum   women
and passing two latterday Quechuanos
hewers of dung   chewers of cocaine
wandering in some dull symbiosis
(not one of us could hope for)
with their silent herds

Upwards and bright with birds and orchids
the undiscouraged forest reaches
clawing over the great cliffs
at the lowest rockstep
and the tidied fruitless marketplace

By grain   clod   stone
the architrave crumbles   and the hill
The corn terrace sifts to the Urubamba
to the Amazon   joins the attrition
of continents perishing into the sea

Stripped tomb and town of triumph
sooner or later you will finish dying
      like all of us
                        Till then
      it is good and beautiful to see you stare
      out of your green humped cumulus
      of mountains and the human mist   you
      and Hiram Bingham and the high Incas
      obstinately into your Sun

Peru 1962

LETTER TO A CUZCO PRIEST

Father   whose name
your smalltown paper took in vain

Young father   whose face
blurred in the cheap newsprint
I could not recognize in a street

Father   who will never know me
nor read this   which is written
in your honour
in the terms of my worship

Father   forgive yourself

This morning two Quechuanos
tramped on their horny feet
down sun-ravaged slopes
clutching cardboard banners
Thirty more Indians followed
sunfaced   silent   ragged
and as many boneknobbly goats
maybe a hundred sheep
gut-swollen   yammering
Their dust rose   was carried
by thin winds like incense
over sculptured rocks
that once bore up the Moon's Temple

Dry wail of the beasts
dropping over denuded terraces
enchanted the ears of travellers
lining up two Cuzco kids
(dressed like Inca princelings
by the Oficina de Tourismo)
to be shot by cameras
in front of the Bath of the Priestess

Father   worship yourself

Where stony slopes level
to unfenced valleys   the sheep
took over the lead   sniffing grass
not the boundary stakes

Father you were not with those shepherds
but your Word sent them

A local watchman for the Lima agent
for the American banker
for the Peruvian landowner
living in Madrid

phoned the Cuzco cops
who phoned the army regiment
quartered locally to handle such jobs

Father   the guilt is not yours
though words that blazed last week
from your pulpit lettered their placards

The two who bore them are dead

Father   the guilt begins
in the other pulpits and all the places
where no one will say your words

"The Government is only
an armed front for Fifty Families"

where no one calls on whatever his country

"Let the land feed its people"

Father   the guilt is not that you spoke
nor that the poor listened   acted
have come again to defeat

Twenty of those who followed
into convenient range of the troops
tend their own wounds
in the jail's bullpen

Father   forgive all men if you must
but only in despite of god
and in Man's name

Their flocks   driven back
to the spiny heights
are herded now by the boys and women

Do not forgive your god
who cannot change   being perfect

    Blood dries on the uncropped grass
    The goats eat dust

Father   honour your Man,
though he will not honour you
in whatever priestly purgatory
authority muffles you now

    In Cuzco the paper that quoted the sermon
    and printed your face
    today demands death
    for the Red (Indian?) spies in the Andes

Father   gullible and noble
born to be martyred
and to be the worthy instrument
of the martyrdom of the gullible

    I who am not deceived
    by your cold deity

    believe

    for there is no other belief

    in the wild unquenchable God
    flaming within you

Pray to yourself above all for men like me
that we do not quench
the man
in each of us

Cuzco 1962

BUENOS AIRES: 1962

Gentes de las esquinas
de pueblos y naciones que no están en el mapa—
(Rafael Alberti)

Traffic like a smoked ant-nest—
on avenues ampler than the political vision
motorists before rounding the empty Senate
make 120 kph and direct daily contact
with a hundred pedestrians

Alberti, I don't see you on any corner

Pedestrians of course complain in all cities
Even when the sidewalk holes are plugged
they grumble as they trample in the fresh cement
Whether it's from staring at the other sex
or at other goods they can't afford to buy
people simply won't keep their eyes
on the pavement even in misty Buenos Aires

Here however the complainers never protest
to the police   handy as the police are
   ubiquitous in fact as the flowers
   in the ringaround parks
   and almost as exotic
   stamened with handgrenades
   petalled in weaponry
   while with the added mobility
   of the animal world
   they trudge three abreast
   in the reasty gutters

It is of course scarcely shrewd
to approach a uniform
Civil or National   Army Navy or Airforce

Cunningham-Graham, what would you have said?

For if one is a Black
    that is to say a Red
and duty bound to scatter leaflets
around the nidorous slaughterhouses
the problem is to get any dropped
before being approached first   and shot
    by the police (Civil or etc.)
Some Blacks therefore fire first
and scatter after
However   the one who gets shot
is usually the ancient corner newsboy

Lugones, you would have cried out for him

Still   if one is a Red Peronista
    that is, an anti-Red anti-Black
and eligible to attend the University
it may be necessary to distract or bribe
the police (Civil) from sentry stance
outside fusty schools with Jewish children
in order to throw grenades safely
at the children   and so defy the government

There are also people without any colour
who occasionally spit
carefully in no direction
immediately after being passed in a street
    by a brace of police (Anybody's)

Ricardo Molinari, have you spoken of these?

and there are other folk whose possible
existence is discussed in posters
appearing and quickly disappearing
on spattered walls in backstreets
beyond the sleasy grandiosities
of the tourists' quarters
The posters include photos of children
    Where is my poppa? His name is . . .

Police took him away on the night of . . .
Nothing has been heard . . . My mother and I
But these of course must be real communists
i.e. not human   and anyway lying   or dead

Meanwhile in the cathedral
big and gray and intricate as a cruiser
what is left of the body of San Martín
father etc of South American democrepence
crumbles under a Darius-sized mausoleum
In the church porch a scarred old woman
stocks all three of the German dailies
none of which is interested in San Martín

Ocampo, there's more here than a Greek myth

Over the titanic horses
in trickling fountains
the next generation climbs
shooting water pistols   and playing
    at being police (Airforce)

By the shallow Plata   the sea still far away
the police (Naval) play
    at being police too
They guard all approaches to tugboats and barges
and are most intrepid in seizing
tourists' cameras and unlicensed whores

Galvez, who speaks now for these limed girls?

Beyond the parks fortified with statues
and the façades of an ersatz Madrid
lies a square mile of workers' flats
frightfully contemporary   and unfinished
since the workers (who fill the next
square mile   of drunken tin shacks)
have been diverted to priority jobs
erecting the offices for the Offices of Housing

and for the Army Navy Airforce
   and Police (Civil and National)

Neruda, there's only you, the foreigner, saying it

There is also an especially ugly building
where Argentine's statesmen like to meet
It is of course a military club
and grants associate membership
   to officers of the Police (Army, Navy, etc.)

Poets and drones together   on the map's edge
cry for your flat city of lost good airs
largest now of all the human ant-nests
in the halfworld below the equator

Alberti,   "we, all the moored shores of the world
beg you to take us in the deep wake
of your ship, to the sea, our chains broken"

CURAÇAO

I think I am going to love it here

I ask the man in the telegraph office
the way to the bank
He locks up and walks along with me
insisting he needs the exercise

When I ask the lady at my hotel desk
what bus to take to the beach
she gets me a lift with her beautiful sister
who is just driving by in a sports job

And already I have thought of something
I want to ask the sister

1962

SALTFISH AND AKEE

The akee's flower is fat and pallid
too aptly named *Blighia sapida*
for Capt. (Chas. Laughton) Bligh
In his imperial days
white men forced the lacquer pods
died learning not to eat the pulp
when it was green

On Jamaica now the children of the freed
take time for loving
let the black seeds unsheathe themselves
contrive to make the bounty of their pith
glorify a salted cod

My last night on the island
one hostess was a girl whose blood
branched back to Pekin, Dahomey,
Bangalore perhaps
The other   velvetskinned
graceful as a dark gladiolus
served saltfish and akee to us three:

  two pink young Montréal boyfriends
  one graywhite Vancouver me

The cod was from Newfoundland   they said
The new found land is here   I said

Port Royal 1962

PROFESSOR OF MIDDLE ENGLISH CONFRONTS MONSTER

Sitting under my almond tree shield
I'm aware that something like a dragon
—rampant   *or* in a *vert* field—
affronts me from a limb

Suddenly under his ambiguous chin
he puffs up a large bag
—lozenge of vellum *blanc*—
then lets it out again

Not a drakish muscle moves in the light
yet he eyes me—is it with bale?—
swells it   deflates it
uncaring as—
    as a subteenager
    blowing bubblegum

I wonder what
St. George would have done

University of the West Indies 1962

CARIBBEAN KINGDOMS

Flowers live here as easily as air
They hang from power lines   they grow on light
A scalloped leaflet lying on a stair
will puff pink buds   and root itself in stone—
The animal hunts by day or pads within the night

The waxy jasmine   Indian arum   red mimosa
tangle unbruised   thigh to alien thigh
the dark Ashanti Blood   the yellow roses
keep peace beneath a prism sun—
White men alone the rainbow world deny

Stubborn as coral the crimson flowers rise
The torch plant towers higher than a man
Each dawn hibiscus gaze with newmade eyes
and cereus nightly stars the jungle roof—
The other kingdom rules what roosts it can

Petal and bract outdo the stir of sky
Their silent cockatoos in every park
preen and are fed without the need to fly
Coldly they nourish birds of heat   and shelter
all bony forms that cry before the dark

Still souls of butterflies the orchids poise
about the flaming trees and are not singed
Lilies turn spiders into spirit   dragons to toys
The Passion Flower lifts its crucifix unmanned—
Only the worlds of blood on suffering are hinged

When all the life of sound has milled
to silence I think these vines will find
a way to trumpet green and purple still
and jacarandas ring their bells down ruined streets—
Our kingdom comes and goes with mind

Mona, Jamaica 1962

TRANSISTOR

She clung to the broom
a long witchy affair she'd been using
to swipe the ancient floor
of the one habitable room
when we came in for a breather
out of the jeep and the humid morning
to this guesthouse
where no one stayed any more
Eyes too bright to be plumbed
gleamed above the homemade handle
She was just tall enough to see over
and her arms   from the grip of the hands
were torsioned as burnt tree-roots

"Like she was hol'in a mike"
the engineer's little black steno said
and giggled   drifting then to the porch
where her boy friend already had vanished
They had come along for the ride

But the old woman was belting songs out
as if she had to send them all the way
back to the sea and the canebrakes
her greatgrandfather ran from
the night he brought her words
stored in his rebellious head
beyond the howl of the slavers' hounds
to this remotest hilltop in Jamaica

In truth she'd never faced mike nor tape
Today was the first she'd seen a transistor
and she'd stared at that more with fear
than interest when the little steno
had sauntered by from the jeep with it

An anchor to keep the rest of her tiny self
from floating up level with the notes
was more what she needed the broom for
I thought   utterly stilled in my chair
under the clean power
coiled in four generations of skulls
and springing out now
from the mouth of this bird-still body

It was the engineer she sang for
because he had asked her
he always did
Yet mine was a new face
with the colour to make anyone wary
up in these mountains
So she stood poised for reversal
back to the caretaker's role

But she soon forgot me   him too
as her mind unravelled to airs
a grandmother might have woven
stooping in dappled coffee groves
when this was a plantation house
buzzing with whiteman's prospering

She paused only once   to down a glass
the engineer poured from the rum he'd brought
He knew what songs to ask for
and out they came now whorling
as if her voice were immortal and separate
within her   and she only the toughened reed
vibrated still by the singing dead
by the slaved and the half-free
The narrow high-ceilinged room was a box
resounding with all the mourning of loves
and deaths   the fear of Mamba   hope of Jesus
the bitter years and the bawdy
till suddenly   at her first falter
she seemed to listen
and stopped

It was not quite all
though my thanks alone might have sent her off
if the engineer hadn't silently offered
a second rum   The besom again in one hand
like a rifle at ease
she swung to me
and in the grave high rhythms of the Victorians
toasted my health
and that of all the gentlemen of my nation
with all the dignity of hers
then disappeared into her kitchen
broom already waggling

It was only then I let my ear tell me
there'd been a counter-bass going on all along
Out on the dusty porch I found the young pair
sitting on the rail at the farthest corner
Two faces black and anxious
leant together under the transistor
They'd found a nail in a pillar to hang it by
The morning disc spin from Puerto Rico
was sending a Hollywood cowboy
from last year's Parade
The machine swung his voice from shriek
to silence and back
I suppose they'd been listening to him
as exclusively as I to her
and out of just as much need
to exchange our pasts

Yallahs Mountain 1962

FOR GEORGE LAMMING

To you
    I can risk words about this

Mastering them   you know
    they are dull
        servants
who say less
    and worse
        than we feel

That party above Kingston Town
    we stood   five (six?) couples

linked singing
    more than rum happy

I was giddy
    from sudden friendship
wanted   undeserved

    black tulip faces

self swaying forgotten

    laughter in dance

Suddenly on a wall mirror
    my face assaulted me
stunned to see itself
    like a white snail
        in the supple dark flowers

Always now I move grateful
        to all of you
who let me walk thoughtless
        and unchallenged
in the gardens
        in the castles
                of your skins

Off Haiti 1962

MEETING OF STRANGERS

"Nice jacket you got dere, man"

He swerved his bicycle toward my curb
to call   then flashed round the corner
a blur in the dusk   of somebody big
redshirted   young   dark   unsmiling

As I stood hoping for a taxi to show
I thought him droll at least
A passing pleasantry?   It was frayed
a sixdollar coat   tropical weight
in this heat only something with pockets
to carry things in

Now all four streets were empty
Dockland   everything shut

It was a sound no bigger than a breath
that made me wheel

He was ten feet away   redshirt
The cycle leant by a post farther off
where an alley came in   What?!

My turning froze him
in the middle of some elaborate stealth
He looked almost comic   splayed
but there was a glitter
under the downheld hand
and something smoked from his eyes

By God if I was going to be stabbed
for my wallet (adrenalin suffused me)
it would have to be done in plain sight
I made a flying leap
to the middle of the crossing
White man   tourist   surrogate   yes
but not guilty enough
to be skewered in the guts for it
without raising all Trinidad first
with shouts   fists   feet   whatever
—I squared round to meet him

and there was a beautiful taxi
lumbering in from a sidestreet
empty!

As I rolled away   safe as Elijah
lucky as Ganymede
there on the curb I'd leaped from
stood that damned cyclist solemnly
shouting

"What did he say?"   I asked the driver
He shrugged at the windshield
"Man dat a crazy boogoo
He soun like he say
'dat a nice jump you got too' "

Port-of-Spain 1962

CARACAS

Pumped up
        from the immigrant ships
by the great hose of the American-aid Hiway
        labourers
homesick for marginal bogs
        in Galicia
lengthen the 9-mile ooze
        of slums
(2 walls of packingbox   2 walls of air)
(1/2 a scraptin roof)
from which fountain 89 highrisers

Drowned
        in the cement foam
rests the National Pan-
        theon
with the 206 bones of Bolívar

Limber as sharks   1,000 Cadillacs   twist
round the submerged reefs of the Capitol
        where 1 declaration of independence
is said to lie
        encrusted in a bronze urn
They swim upwards then
        through shoals
            of Galicians
and the rest of the 7,000,000
        lesser organisms
towards the bright bloodsmell
        of dollar$$$
lapping hotels like beached liners
        on the airwashed atolls
            of America's Venezuela

1962

TURBONAVE MAGNOLIA

The padre with the penguin's belly
    and the one-eyed purser
        have finished cheating us out of a few pesetas
            by signals we never could quite make out
        based on the patterns of stacking
—or the speed or pitch of slapping?—
dominoes on an arborite table

My partner is now pouring again
    his pint milkbottlefull of pale gravel
        on the top of the Cabin bar
            which we are allowed to visit
                from the Other Class
                    This time it's the coiffeuse from Caracas
                        going back to Spain for a husband
                            who sees fortune's bright rope of sand
                        spinning out from my partner's wrist
                    The limber finger of the ex-bank-clerk
                is piecing out bits of the Essequibo riverbed
            and pointing at not-quite-diamonds
        while the other hand scratches his lank thigh,
rummaging independently among jungle sores

The *Magnolia* suddenly
                catches herself by her ancient
                throat
            shudders up and down both her Classes con-
        vulses   forward   again
        as the propellor once more manages to find
            the sea

Weaving back alone to the Other Saloon
   I have my first drink of the day
      a *tinto corriente* with a mussel-dark
         fish-pedlar sailing forever from Georgetown
     to the Empire's heart   to Paddington
   where his brother has a job for him
cleaning up in the fish market

We talk about last night's ruckus
     between a Galician steward (Cabin)
       and a creole passenger (Other)
         over a close call at bingo
      the steward was souzled but had the help
   of a Canario deckman who led with a fast
right foot to the jaw and won
We agree that the deckman knew how to time
   his jumps with the heave of the ship
     the pedlar tells me the Valencian waiter
       reappeared this morning   a deckswabber now
         He singin but man you cooda see dem scratches!
      That China gel he lep on dat firs day out—
    You dint heah man?   Yeh yeh in her cabin
   He hop in wen she nursin her pickney
No she still nuff sick in her bert!

Clowning in and out of the bow waves
   porpoises are trying to entertain
     the Entertainment Officer who gazes beyond them
       solemn as ever   perhaps at the thundercaps
         which look as black as the two that suddenly
        moved in to a fury of spat and whirl last night
      while he gravely carried on with a second showing
   (free and deafening, for all Other passengers)
of a Hollywood film about a great liner
   that goes assoverkettle hissing down in a gale
     when haughty officers panic   I walk out and ask him?
       Si, tonight   third showing   but for Cabin only. . . .

Anyway we've had lifeboat drill
  It was the third day out and everybody
    even Cabin   herded into Our eating space
      while the boats were searched and found
      empty of stowaways but full of rainwater
    Both classes were then permitted
  on production of tickets
to march back to their separate bingo games

I am deck-strolling now with an Oxford graduate
  who sold a good business in Tobago
    to be a socialworker in Liverpool
      We discuss the trapping of cockroaches in cabins
        and how to contrive to eat together
        for he sleeps in Cabin   being flush
      and I in Other   being other
    but he eats in Other   being gravybrown-skinned
  and I in Cabin Early Sitting   being potato-white
We call on the Chief Steward and get a final brush-off
Eat together? !   This is the one improbability.

Off Tenerife, December 1962

TO A HAMILTON (ONT.) LADY THINKING TO TRAVEL

Should you stop in Barranquilla?
My anxious lady   what for?
It's just another polluted port
a little larger but not quite as ugly
and as you say
all cities are much—
foundries breweries asylums universities
tankers pill-factories
And perhaps if you wait long enough
in Hamilton
you'll hear your own cabbies
honk three bars of Strauss
before attacking a pedestrian
and municipal busses   blow
(2¢ anywhere, turkeys free)
the toreador song

Give us all enough time
& warmer winters
& maybe we'll all be shopping barefoot
for hash in the farmers' market
your husband with long braids
snaking down his gathered skirt

Yes indeed much warmer winters
& you'll see pedlars
come shouting right here down King Street
spidermonkeys swirling round their necks
and small boys padding naked from the harbour
dangling twofoot sharks
to flog in the supermarket
No mam if i were you
i'd just stay put in Hamilton
Ont.

1963

1968: Australia & New Zealand

A SMALL FACULTY STAG FOR THE VISITING POET

but a large quantity of brandy
                    on whisky
                    on sherry

At one table's end the Necessary Dean
has broken out cigars
At the other the Oxonian Canon
splotchfaced now
is putting us all down with naughty quotes
from Persius we're too slow to get
—except the Czech professor & the Hungarian
who dig everything
so civilised they're savage with disappointment
in us all & no doubt saying so this moment
safely across my chest in at least 2 languages

somewhere in the smoke the Librarian
is heard toasting the cummunwealth
& feck the Yenks
The Padre winces & gradually
like Yahweh in the Zohar withdraws his presence
leaving behind that vacuum of Evil
which is us

The Physics Department's chief cultural exhibit
also a very anthropologetical Native Son
have just asked me unanswerable questions
simultaneously from across the centrepiece

I am the dead eye of this verbal typhoon
I am the fraudulent word-doctor
stripped to dumbness by their tribal ritual
I am neither civilised nor savage but also Necessary

          grinning
          & stoned
          & desolate

Australia 1968

THE 21ST CENTURY BELONGS TO THE MOON

northeast from the Alice
Australia's attic
a tundra in reverse
arctic-flat & rimless
offwhite and empty as Keewatin
but this one's permaroasted

on a wart of rock like Yellowknife
nowhere a now town
chewing an upshove of ore
its lifelines ruled by planes
that fly-in whole mine-rigs
highriser assemblies
& once an orchestra
for the college wife of an outsider boss
a year is a sentence
thru space into space

my hotel's a set from a western
it leapt here ten years ago from another mine
500 miles of nothingness & north away

the midnight Vulcans come sweating up
playing touchtag along the dark verandahs
before belching into bunks
with Sydney pinups

at dawn the morning shift
explodes in my ear
no flight till sundown
what to do?

under the sign

      DRINKS SERVED ONLY IN BULLPEN

i quiz the desk-clerk

      eyent nuffink ear fer tewrists, myte
      cept myebee a gyme at the grensten

i follow his landmarks past

      AUSTRALIA'S BIGGEST RODEO
      (thet wuz ite months ago, myte)

to a halo of dust in the morning
whirling from longjawed miners' kids
locked in rugger (aussie rules)
in the stand a bigboned mother
calls ritually to her son

      kickim inniz kinneez wenease dahn!

wandering back
i am suddenly in silence
& a levelled vacancy
bared rock circled by spinifex
no habitations
only this metal shaft
centring nothing
etched symbols glow in the fierce sun
unsigned
unspoken of

this pillar haunts
will haunt me
like Kubrick's in 2001
the sky's blue is hard as bakelite
on all sides the reefs of alkali
stretch white like icefloes
turning in space

Mount Isa, Queensland 1968

PERTH, AUSTRALIA, I LOVE YOU

Who wouldnt
after rocking 2000 miles over the Nullabor
in a series of giant prams
each a different gauge   but all permawaved
2000 miles *sans arbres sans* leaf or life?

& then   Greenness—ah Perth my lovely!

True your suburbs look as dull as Edmonton's
& rotting stumps commemorate great trees
tall as Vancouver's were   forever lost
& oil creeps up Freemantle sands
& the World is rapidly coming to an End

but meantime here's You in your September spring
a launching pad for botanists on space-trip
a happening in spice & rainbows
a young witch gardening
between Outback & empty Ocean
growing Everybody's Posies
from iceland poppies to jungle orchids
& 300 species of acacia

   we callem wottles, myte

& blue-blue dampiera & groovy guinea flowers
under old Charles Darwin's palms
& those crazy petalled creatures totally your own
with sadsack names

   cockies' tongues & kangaroo paws

or labelled like rare diseases

pink mulla mulla   backhouse correa

Ah Perth you tight little city
you tropical Kensington
with a duplicate Peter Pan where picknickers meet
before chugging off to Rot-Nest Island
to hunt rat-roos
Perth with *His* Majesty's Theatre on Hay St.
picketed by stern patriots
warning off Moseyev's ballet dancers
from reddening the Last White Continent
Perth i love you despite you
i'm with your surf   your surfers
the ritualistic lifeguards

your treasured temples: the first Mill
the second Brewery   the crafted home
wild Tom Collins built & i yawped my poems in

Perth i dig even your "Uni"
though no one likes universities any more
Who wouldnt be turned on by a campus
where wild parrots shriek at deans
from figtrees & the only fuzz patrolling
campus beaches grows on wild black swans
& the academic groves conceal a footlong dinosaur
stumptailed & sunset-mottled
Trachysaurus rugosus   (the gardener says

    jus wot we call a ly-zee lizza
    wen eyewuzza kid yewzabee orrana beckyahds)

Perth you unchartable & knowing creature
it's your poets send me most of all
Hail Dorothy exmillworker prof   & mother of 5
coffee-house reader   greatboned & hearted!
Hi Merv your bigger husband!
walking from bush-school to cane-cutting at 13
& now the world's lone poet
with a lawn-mowing syndicate!
Towering like karri trees
you bring the young beneath your shelter
open your home & arms to droppers-out
young dogs & rebels & old loonies like me
to throw an intermedic Eisteddfod
on the farthest Perthian rim
of our unheeding planet

PERTH you pink mulla mulla take me back
Why did i ever leave you?

West Australia 1968

MUSEUM OF MAN

the trustful curator has left me alone
in the closed wing of the aboriginal section

what's here?
3000 spears from arnhemland
waiting for a computer
to calculate their principle of balance

but what's in those wooden drawers?
i peek—sheeeez! shrunken heads
from new guinea
& dozens upon dozens
of twelve-inch penis sheathes

i'm going to lock doors
plant spears at windows
& try on everything for size

Adelaide 1968

TODAY'S YOUR BIG PUBIC READING

A giant is banging on my door
crikes it's only seven thirty
He's clashing dungeon keys
He's wrenched the lock off
before i can shout guhway—
hell it's only the same bantam chambermaid
bearing my tea
tepid and sugared
prim-lipt in
and prim-assed out

and back i'm rolling
to hours of lovely suhleeep
below the guttering of summer rain
when some superegoistic
devil in my skull
begins to shout
GET UP!   REMEMBER YESTERDAY
YOU GOT DOWN AFTER EIGHT
(*Who cares?*)
YOU DO!
COLD TOAST AGAIN
AND NOTHING ELSE
(*doanwanennythinelse*)
GET UP!   you need your STRENGTH—
TODAY'S YOUR BIG PEWBIGREADING
(*asnottle three*)
HA!
YOU GOT *A SEMINAR AT TEN A.M.*!

fumbling up
i'm sick in the basin
hot water's colder
than what's droning down outside
goddamit nobody
but nobody
ever warms australian hotels
kin i havenlectric heater in my room?
   a wot?
   aow naow
   ent naow pattables jes nah

once i blasted stumps
i'm testing the fumes again—
i've got flu!
must be asian
india's the next place north
GET DOWN TO BREAKFAST!

the lift is stuck
i wobble down three flights
too late for anything
except a morning paper
MOVE, MAN!
Expectant i paw it
standing now in a lake
waiting for the Public Transport
while my flubug mounts a needle
to probe my left tonsil

four miles by abomnibus
and dripping all the way
and not one bloody word
about my Reading

ten a.m.
i'm high on virus
Modern British Poets whoops!
what's Mod today?   Dylan?
Bob or Thomas?
gawd it's Masefield
they're deep in
till the last ten minutes—
now my ears are ringing—
    do tell us about Kinnidah
TELL THEM
one chick has heard of Leonard Cohen
    yeh but eeze ammirikin
no!   munreeawl kin-age-in
    aow wail—kin-eye-gin, noaf ammirikin,
    izzola syme

twelve-fifteen
department luncheon all for me
i have tea and aspirins
and learn i'm being joed
to run the Chaucer seminar
from now till three—no!
i need *rest* before my Pughb—
YOU CANT LET CHAUCER DOWN
i'm *old* too
LET ALONE THE CANADA COUNCIL!
i'm going to faint—
GET OFF YOUR ASS!

They're "doing" the *Troilus*
entire in two hours
by modern Coghill
(we dont even speak
the same Chaucerian)
and i am dying
but not from courtly love
there's maggots in my bones

Now i'm sent reeling
down an endless hallway
If i see a First Aid i'll
KEEP GOING
YOUVE COME TEN THOUSAND MILES
ONLY TWENTY YARDS MORE

i grab the UNI NEWS
Faculty Meet at 3 Today
the motherfuckers
that's when i'm to read!
To Consider Curriculum Changes

v

i'm splitting!   i'm RIGHT TURN
THERE'S YOUR DOOR
sure enough
READING OF CANADIAN VERSE
BY E. BARNIE 3 p.m.
my head aches and a lousy dumbness. . . .

Seems i'm the only one
on time
but two Gretchens trail me in—
on mute request
i autograph their notebooks
and they plod out again
the cultural exchange over—
three balding males
file bleakly to the front
(hostages from the Staff in English)
. . . at last the Chairman
leading a squad of youth
who scatter to the back
& sit apart like snipers . . .
i wait out the introduction
wrestling against sneezes
& counting 207 vacant seats . . .
after my first hoarse poem
there are two more empties . . .
twice an angel maiden laughs
but no one joins her
at the right moments . . .
my eyes are blurring
my throat's closing up—BALLS
YOU CANT QUIT NOW
REMEMBER: CANADA MADE YOU

bell rings—it's over!
except for The Reception—No! No!

miracle!—i'm spared
by blessed Sister Nausea
and take my flu back
tenderly in the bus
it really is the Asian

seven-thirty
next morning
the giantess is back
with tea & superego
GET UP!
YOU GOTTA CATCH THE PLANE
No!   *YES!*
YOU GOT ANOTHER PEWBIG
AT WOOLAGONDALONGADONG

Australia 1968

STRINE AUTHORS MEET

No tram   taxi dumps me on wrong side of the unknown
I climb through a maze of academic alleys   5 minutes late
blunder into a middleclass quagmire lapping up sherry

A female macaw beckons me   the local Edith Sitwell?
    Yew the kin eyejin gander gisses a lecher?
    Jus gonna read pomes
Her bill falls with alarm
    Yer nat gander read peartree? Ow long yer gan an fer?
    I allus go on till the chairman stawps me.
    Aow   (she takes my arm firmly)   yid better talk to im

We walk to the table head past place cards for 60   Cripes!
   Ow yea-yes Misser Binney   ow surrey   Misser *Ben*ny
   We been waytin fer yew
I can see the sherry's gone
An ancient fat man he sighs   but affably i think
   Rid semmena yers once about a kin eyejin fren jew add
   was killed at Deeper summers
Before I can figure that out & say thanks he's warning me
   this the Fickle Tree Club   we got to be houtbee tin
   and pipple still kemmenin   wont get stetted til Apis hate
   and henyule meeting kems festive curse
   be lucky tev affenahr fer wotayver yew intindin tew dew

We sit   The muscular arms of the lady on my right
have found a worthy opponent in the chicken
I interrupt her battle to express genuine pleasure
to see so many of the city's authors here tonight
But this one's a realist   modest too   between bites
   Affefems jis spouses   uzbints   woives   or frinze
   loike me   oim only the voice prisidents woif
I ask about the macaw down the table
   ow *err* she roits fiction   nuvvles   foive so far
She told me their names & the macaw's   nothing rang a bell
I'd slipped on my homework   Who was her publisher?
   Ow aint nennem peblished   but she's read em all to us

Nine already & still eating   Not being warned
my show was private i'd asked my young friend M
for the reading   By now he must be wandering the campus too
I told the chairman   who hadnt heard of M or of his book
(last year's winner of the national first-novel prize)
   Allem seats is pied in idvence   an allem sowld
   (He smiled) Sivn dollars a plight   Yer ena trek shun
The buggers i thought   they got me free   not even tramfare
and begrudge a chickenbone for penniless M
I tell the chairman i'm leaving to find M He shrugs
   Iffey dan moind settin anna floor

I tell him M can have my place   I'll read standing
but just then M comes in deadpan with two young poets
All squat burying their long locks
in the darkest corner

The business drones on to 9.30   when the chairman introduces
a gentleman with a white goatee & stammer   who introduces
Mr. Buh-Beaney   & sits down at 9.45
The chairman huskily reminds me i've only 15 minutes
I decide to dedicate them entirely to the far corner

First a hands-across-the-commonwealth   let's make it
Frank Scott's *The Canadian Authors Meet*: "Expansive puppets
percolate self-unction. . . ."
& now a glimpse of Canada's romantic north: Purdy's piece
about the dangers of shitting among huskies   followed by
a small statement of my own poetics: "how fucking awful
it is to be a poet" & finally a Bill Bissett "hare krishna"
chanted   walking out with the only three writers in the room

Melbourne 1968

THE GRAY WOODS EXPLODING*

(For Vin Buckley, who is not in the story, but helped me straighten my Strine)

(1)

Flying from the dry pall of the city
i watch roads wrinkle   dwindle up the dun Range
& disappear in the general pox
of eucalyptus   the skin of a land
hard & vacant as the faces
of swagmen in Australian painting

(2)

But suddenly all is tressed
with turbulence
violet smoke rocketing up & away to the Tasman—
Fire is loose   wild in a hundred hills
& the gray woods exploding

Somewhere between the red cores
of combustion there must be birds
falling   & screaming horses
in flight from this fearful beauty
marsupials   men   ambushed
each creature whirling away
from the palsied will of the trees
to die & immolate all
in a violence of comets over the quiet sea

(3)

The plane floats untouched
but i hear again that lone ghost-gum in the Olgas
pricked by a campfire spark
roaring to sacrifice
the air filled in an instant with crimson tongues
& the screech & outswoop of parrots

In the time of remembering
i drift beyond sight of perdition
& look down again on mere grayness

Bored & inert as gods we descend   cloudwrapped
to the darkening human valleys

(4)

Morning & a Head of English
a bush of hair drab as old tumbleweed
motors me thru such predictable gridirons
of stuccoed cafés & pumps & beer barracks
i might be back in Albertan foothills
some town with a fringe collegiate
united by yellowing litter   sex

the profit unsystem   & October's wind
mottling the general flesh

But those white splashes are surely not snow
It's spring Down Here & blossoming apples
That *déjà-vu* of an always-too-early fall
was only within me—
or a bleakness breathed by my host
this young-old stranger
confronting me now from his business suit
I sit upright in his office cave
hung round with books like stalactites
& stare into pale eyes   a face ungiving
obscurely scarred
as he runs down my day's obligings

(5)

Now i'm guesting the inevitable seminar:
Eliot of course   with graduate students
A numismatic exhibition   See!
though we live in the Outback
dont our coins ring true as Oxford's?
& we got them all through reliable dealers . . .
I've faced those lacklustre fronts before
at U.B.C   Berkeley   Toronto: *Academicus anaemicus*

Into the usual dismal student caf for sandwiches
The reading follows & some of the faculty come
hear   spare me their feelings
But i caught some young eyes softening with laughter
& i'm starting to ease

(6)

My chairman-host seems easier too
discards his coat for a rollneck
& takes me into the drywine sunlight
We twist up hills in his landrover
smoking our dust into gumtrees
& the ramshackle gates of stations

He's relaxed enough to be quizzing'me
in his diffident way   about Canada
The woods thin into mallee scrub & wanness
while we talk large of our countries' identities
& cautiously then of our own
He's Australian B.A. with a Master's from London
Set up the local department a few years ago
    And before that?
        Umm—many things   none relevant—
        And here's where the road ends

(7)

He means it literally
Leaving the car we tread over leaves like paper
Under a stiff blue sky   & in seconds
stand on a gulf edge—
face blotched by vanished cascades
granite sheering to depths unseeable
like an Andean chasm
We sit dangling our feet over silence
The smell of height stirs me
& i want to go below surfaces
Is there something tight in this man
he cant untie with words   or wont?
I try to trigger his past with my own:
my early jobs as an axeman   housepainter
guide in the Rockies—It works in a fashion:
        Good on you Earle
(at least we've got to first names   i'm no longer Doctor)
        you know what it's like being poor
        & sweating your guts out
(a hint of Strine in the London overlay now)
    You too, Jack—you werent always a prof—
But he jumps up so quickly something   a crow?
squawks from a branch in panic
        Too roight!   but it's time we're back
        I'll shout you a beer at the motel
        & then we'll feed at my place
        if you'll risk a bachelor's tucker

(8)

I accept quickly & we turn to the rover
Casually he gestures back at the gorge
    A mate of mine came here once—
    to jump off   Changed his mind
    Said it queered his pitch
    not seeing ahead where he'd land
The flatness of tone belies any joke
I search those darting eyes
They are leafgreen now but still unbetraying
    You cant stop there! What's the story?

He climbs to the wheel with a low laugh
    You'd find it boring   & it hasnt an ending

(9)

But grudgingly almost he sketches it in
as we bump down through the slaty gums
their trunks radiant now in the slant light
    We can call him Pat
    A fatherless kid from the slums   so he said
    on his own early   a slygrogger's runner
    (bootlegger's boy maybe you'd call it
    you'll have to pardon the argot
    but profs' lingo wont do here)
    So then he was copped for theft
    & jailed in what they still call a Boys' Home
    School for larrikins rather   for making young thugs

    Well he learned to drive a cat there at least
    broke out   stole new clobber—clothes—duds do you say?
    hitched north   took a new nime
    & got a job stripping coral from the Barrier Reef
    It was a Yank oil company
    & the moolah was good
    but he left it & went on the bum

When i asked why   his voice went oddly brusque
    How should I know? Just a dopey kid
    Got wet maybe—blew his top—or started to think
    what a bloody thing that was
    to do to the Great Barrier Reef

Jack busied himself with the driving then
till i prodded him on
    Ah it's just more of the sime
    He bummed   mainly off sheilas
    popped rabbits   went fossickin   quit
    Got a good set-up then   bulldozing bauxite
  And he left it in no time—
He shoots me almost a frightened look

    How'd you know?
  Because it was a bloody thing to do to beaches
  Your Pat was an idealist
    Was he?
    Maybe he just didnt like
    spitting out blood with aluminum
He turns his head & his eyes are flecked
He is nettled   I'm being bumptious
    No offense Jack   i forgot he was someone close—
    Close? what do you mean by that?
    Look   dont worry   he's not here now
The laugh is friendly   but he pushed the gas
as we bounce in sight of the straggling town
    Hell I shouldnt have started this
    It was only because you're a visiting fireman
  I wont retail it—but i would like to hear the rest!
    Over the suds then maybe   We'll make for your motel
    I'm perishin thirsty

(10)

We pry a pair of schooners out of the deafening "public"
& set them between us up in my room
I fill him in by request on Canadian liquor control
& persuade him at last back to his story
      Well after the bauxite it seems he went droving
      (cattle   that was)   & chucked it
      to be a jackeroo somewhere near Adelyde
      But before that he was up in The Alice I think
      & maybe then he worked as a shearer's rouseabout
      & hunted crocs out from Darwin
      Everywhere you can be sure he drank too much
      & got into fights with his flash temper   quit
      He was a barmy bastard for sure
      & crook in the head

  I dont believe you really think he was
      No?   well he was a bastard   fair dinkum
      & barmy enough to fake still another identity
      & use it to join the bloody rozzers

Who? the police?!   But how could he swing it?
      He'd brines of a sort   read a lot
      managed to scrape through the tests
      was posted into a Sinney suburb
      Liked it   he said   & after a bit he was given a rise
      Yeh he was even up for a medal
I *said* he was an idealist!   How did it happen?
      Idealist? What does it mean? Is it a dirty word?
      I'm just telling you what a man did   or was done to
      He ran through burning bush
      & saved a boy cut off in a shack
      So he was a one-day hero   then he got sacked
      or took off   or both really
Sacked! But why?
      Well the blaze had been set
You mean—a pyromaniac?

No   *entrepreneurs*:   looters
    Didnt you know? that's how most bushfires get started
How do they pull it off?
    One cove starts it   & then pisses off
    The rest of them wait for the panic to start
    move in with unmarked lorries
    & mike out theyve been sent to help
    They load up the family treasures
    & rev off in the smoke
My God that too was happening below!

But was Pat involved in the looting?
    No   but all the other cops were
    Pat was the rookie who didnt know
    & just before he went into the shed for the boy
    he'd recognised a local lout with the truckers
    So he passed the bloke's name to his sergeant
    who came to see Pat in the hospital
    The sergeant was in on the fix naturally
    He gave Pat a chance to share in the tike
    But the idiot blew his top & threatened to go to the press
    The sergeant countered he'd reason to think
    Pat's papers were phony   It was a stand-off
    Pat just took to the road again.
    —& it's time we did too: i'm stahvin'

(11)

We drive through darkening suburbs
to a porchlit cube of stucco
& walk through a scraggly hedge
Behind is dead grass with a small waratah
lifting its quiet bonfire of bloom in the dusk

Then the blank house-door opens into a livingroom
so jumping with strangeness & colour
i'm mortified again at my own failure
to foresee this professor's complexity
The walls flicker with ochre coils
aboriginal paintings on bark   & Namatjiras

Drysdales   a good Piper (from London days?)
Javanese batiks   colour photos of seasnakes & Darwin eagles
Scattered around the floor between ferns
some strangely infolded sculpture

He has a housekeeper after all
an original Australian   ancient creased & gentle
We follow her past a piano (with open music)
to savory food & wine as dry & subtle
as the man who drinks it with me
After we've settled over our pipes in his study
(surrounded by Melbourne playbills & photos of Aussie poets)
& settled the fate of the Commonwealth
& discussed the sculpture   (his own)
Jack comes back to his tale
It seems Pat found enough forms in police desks
to fake a more useful *curriculum vitae*
He hitched & "sundowned" till he'd put a thousand miles
between the past & himself
Then with the last of his money
he enrolled in a university
        A girl in one of his classes fell for him
        They were married & she worked to put him through
        He got a degree & a Nuffield to—ah to Cambridge

Jack gets up abruptly & stalks to the brandy tray
        So after a few years he turned up on our staff
        & well—as I said—we got to be cobbers   sort of
        And that's how I know his story
        Scarcely an idealist eh? A roughneck I'd call him
        with nothing to skite about
        except his incredible luck—
        And now what about a nightcap
        before I take you back to your motel?
I said thanks but reminded him he still hadnt told me why
        Why?   O—the bloody cliff!
        Cant you guess?   The past caught up again
        &—well we've all got lots to grizzle about

He is still fiddling with the drinks
      It was our Uni's Registrar plyed the Fury this time—
Jack seems blocked   His voice falters
He comes back silently with the brandies
his face a sallow mask
      Then Pat's wife   well he was crazy about her
      And there werent any kids
      She'd just died of cancer   That was the boomer

The professor sits   lifts his glass   gestures a toast
      Well that's it   I warned you
His voice swings from dryness to something like anguish
      There's no story   He hadnt the guts to jump
      Anyway there was no need   as it turned out
      The University brass proved frightfully kind & discreet
      kept mum about everything   even found him a job
      in one of the new colleges   a long way off
      So he's still alive   in a way   somewhere
      a good enough teacher   with no ambition
      nobody worries him   perhaps he wont drop out this time
      ideal eh?   but not idealistic—

He gulps the rest of his glass & stands
The laconic tone is back   & the sombre laugh
      Never told that sleeper before   & wont again
      Now how about you? You must be tired
      & your plane goes out damned early
      I'll drive you back for some sleep

I get up slow   asking myself what he wanted to say
The silence   the leaden face   are no longer bearable
I hear myself mumbling
   Still alive   somewhere?   I think I *know* where
It's the wrong gambit   His face suffuses
till the scars of his burns stand blackly out
      It's nobody's fucking business where!
      Dont imagine I've been telling you *my* life   *Doctor*!—
      Whining & whipping the cat—!

We've come face to face   His eyes are flint & sparked with fire
But the next second he's turned
his voice heavy with pale apologies i try bleakly to match

(12)

We step into a chill night without moon
Through a thin cloud-cover the stars are small & dingy
I am driven quickly back   He's the calm Head once more
Our talk exchanges routine assurance & wish
The airport bus will pick me up   His goodbye hand is firm

I stand outside the motel till his car disappears
Over a smudge of treetops   in a cloud-rift
the heaven reveals strange patterns i've yet to learn
I turn to go in   a meteor flashes
brightens to fireball   in a second burns out
It does not startle   I think i'd looked up
expecting it   out of such skies

Australia 1968/Barclay Street, Vancouver 1973

*Warning to all *literalati*: this poem's story is an invention. Pat & Jack are not
based on "actual" people, living or dead. Even the "i" is only half ali(v)e.

CHRISTCHURCH, N.Z.

I have just flown 1100 miles from Australia
& landed in a Victorian bedroom
They sent up cindered muttonchops for lunch
There is an elderly reporter in my room with pince-nez
He wants to know why I have sideburns
& if I dont think being patronized by the Canada Council
isnt dangerous for my art or dont I feel I need to suffer?
In stone outside my window Capt. Scott
is nobly freezing to death near the South Pole
Suddenly I know the reporter is right
Sideburns have been sapping my strength

1968

KIWIS

Up there in Canada we might say weirdo   or screwball
Down under here it's weird bird   pronounced weed bed
Strange phrase for a put-down   considering the emblem
of New Zealand: a wingless tailless chicken
feathered shagreen & shaggy   & breathing through the far-end
of a 6-inch macaroni tube   Still   the oddest birds
are human any place   & hunted by other humans
the Even Ones (in New Zild: the Vest Mejerrty)

That night I was to give a public reading on z campus
Its English Department in the afternoon received me
standing for sweet sherry   & sitting down to bitter tea
Three departmental poets kindly autographed their books
(I'd brought)   & then they left   regretting
they wouldnt hear me since they were reading their own poems
at the same hour in another building

I was meditating how to outploy that exit
when the Head asked me in dulcet Oxcam to explain
what rally does go on in those creetive-writing-shops-
ay-think-you-call-them I told him what went on in mine
then Miss MacSomeone   a small termagant
whose 5 wheelbroken Chaucer students I'd already met
explained that New Zild students were fay too serious
to fend tem for thet   we've British stendids you see
though Ay could quite believe thet in Amirrica . . . I left

Out in the dim hall a bearded youth beset me
Please just *look* at them   he jabbed a scribbler at my chest
& flipped pages   his eyes still probing mine defiantly
Masses of pencilled verse   but sketches too   His gaze
was almost evil   For a moment I was back on the dark stairs
of the Clichy Metro buying a feelthy packet that later
proved to be postcards of statues in the Louvre
But lord these were no fakes   good audiovisuals
shapomes in Swiss and Brazilian contemporary modes
Tim was just old enough I could take him off for a beer

It seems he had a girl in London who sent him Little Mags
He planned to join her but was still in debt to shrinks
after a breakdown when he was flunked out from the U
flunked by one of the 3 tame canaries in the English Dept.
They ole think Oim bonkers   he whispered over the bar table
(as if we were really Underground)   But he thought I'd dig him
I dug   then asked him why the local bards had cut me out
Ah he said   it's cause the Ead asked D to be yer Cheermin
Cripes! I said   he's my friend   & your best-known poet!
Thet's ovaseas   here they think *they're* tops Tim said
& D's been divorced & publishes settires in the dylies
He eynt square enough for them   Ha! I said I see
D's a weird bird!   Roit said Tim   a weed bed loike me
loike you too   Check! I said   & we had another beer

Next day at the zoo I saw my first live kiwi
A young keeper brought it tucked underneath his arm
like Anne Boleyn's head   It wasnt much more animate
He placed it on the announced area of grass & time
the zoo's P.A. had been promising the sky all day
It promptly whacked its long nosebill in the turf
& froze   hunchbacked   splaylegged   shuteyed
while the keeper (quietly in love with the creature)
explained it was a nightbird   shy under flashbulbs
(there were I'd say about 30 cameras clicking)

I think myself with his long schnozzle that kiwi
was quietly turning on to audiovisual worms
wriggling stubborn underneath New Zealand's Weed Bed soil.

1968

1968-1969: South Pacific

ATOLL

Some women's combs are turtleback
glowing like brown moths
in the dusk of their hair
but the heads of the younger chicks
are starred in duraluminum
Their boyfriends
who dive for pearlshell
the only export
hammer out the stars
from Yankee bomberskin
A Liberator crashed in '45
—its crew mistook the torches
of nightfishing dugouts
for an airstrip somewhere else

The Polynesians here add up to 685
There is no census for the shellfish
or the tortoise
Surely there'll be enough plane carapace
to stretch until the next
liberator
At least that's what all the turtles murmur
The oysters as usual say nothing

But some believe the great pearl
in the sky will
some night
fall

Aliepata, West Samoa 1968

SMALL PORT IN THE OUTER FIJIS

Knotheaded men in seaboots all the way from Hokkaido
crowded on a moored fishtank built like a tug
Theyve been catching tuna for rice
& sharks for the fun & fins drying on the rigging now
along with swords of swordfish
Down the scale-slippery wharf
come tippytoe
the new nobility of Fiji:
    Chief Cannery in impeccable shorts
    & Mrs. Sato
    his 1-1/2 size lady
    to greet the Sea Chief
    Tunaboat Captain Moto
    & bear him to their hill villa
    for ceremonial rum & saki
    with the Paramount Chiefs:
        the Aussie Prince of Port
        & the New Zild Lord of Fishmeal
    The Captain Hero will sing them his voyage:
        A full catch before Pango
        but spoiled & sold for catfood
        The present cargo prime but almost confiscated
        when they fished inside the Tonga limits
        But the Captain cut his lines in time
        & said they'd come for water
    Everybody agrees the tuna scarcer
    Korean boats all over
    but fear of mercury keeps down the demand

The sweaty sailors meantime are heaving the great fish
one by one from hold to deck to wharf to truck
Some are hoping there'll be time before sailing
to find a Yankee beer   & even a halfcaste schoolgirl
at the one whorehouse up the one street

The British are all back in Suva
plotting to set Fiji free
The Indians are keeping the shops   & procreating

There are no Fijians in view.

Koro Sea 1969

CUCARACHAS IN PARADISE

I pull out a drawer to get my toothbrush—
kee-rye!   there's a 3-inch monster eating it
A fragment of bristle lies on the lining
(a page from an old *Fiji Times*
half-shredded too   what a digestion)
As I lean near he freezes
watching me somehow
from under the dark oval of his carapace
Some kind of shiny beetle?   vaguely fam—
flash!   at the first twitch of my arm
vanished thru that tiny crack at the back!
(how does he *do* it?)
leaving a cloud of suspicion   an outhouse whiff
over my hairbrush too
A cockroach sure   I'd seen plenty
but they were brown smallfry
scuttling in the lobbies of Toronto walkups
in Basque bedrooms or haunting
pissoirs in Nice, Tv sets in Manhattan
but this was something for Asimov
a sci-fy mutant smoothly taking us over
I shouted for Fred the patron

He's Tahitian   half-French   the logical half
makes his trips on reality
gets really high on atheism
       "Granted   *msieu Birnee*   a cockroach
       even here in Levuka
       the genus is planet-wide   In my Legion days
       they followed us across the Sahara"
"Riding their own camels I'll bet"
       "That I did not see *msieu*
       In Fiji it is clear they grow large
       but you must know that a mere million years ago
       one species extended half a metre at least
       However none will bite you"
"You know damn well Fred these things are—are filthy"
       "*C'est vrai*   *un moment*
       I am fetching my can of airèsol"

After ten minutes Alua found it for him
& he was back vaguely spraying the porch wall
my bureau   my slippers

       "A special mix *msieu*   Fine Mist & choloridane
       it wont kill them quickly   what will?
       but they will perhaps mistake it for an *apéritif*
       when they begin eating the wallpaint & the wood
       both of which they like
       Ah how cheaply we could live
       if we had such assimilation
       if we could treat toothbrushes
       (& your paste too I see)
       as merely desserts"
"*Apéritifs*" I snorted "So what they do for tablewine:
smoke pot? (Fred looked blank)
You know like those cucarachas in Mexico?"
He did not blink   His pale eyes
had come alight with science
       "Let us leave folktales aside & I will tell you:
       just once I left my inkwell uncovered
       I found it dry & two bugs beside it"

"Dead?" I had to ask   Fred shot a jet under the bed
    "Non msieu   but very drunk
    I think for them ink is a *cognac"*
I slid him the rattan stool & lay back on my hammock
Fred sank clutching his weapon   He was just starting:

    "C'est merveilleux n'est-ce pas
    how *adaptable* these roaches?
    Leathers & woods for *entrées*
    my white paint by choice for sauce
    But my spray you see   it taste for them like piss
    (which is their true *vin ordinaire* you ask about)
    They like it too much   They die of *alcoölisme*
    If one could afford enough to spray everything
    all would go . . . us too perhaps" (he shrugged)
"But arent there *safer* ways?
faster ones anyway   As you know
soon I must return to Canada"   Fred got up
    "Une question interessante   oui
    et ayant des raisons suffisantes msieu"
He tiptoed back beside my haunted bureau
one hand on can
wrenched the other topdrawer wide open
There were two even bigger & blacker
dining on the guesthouse's one Gideon Bible
—spplssht! he got them for an instant in his jet
before they split into their fourth dimension
Fred handed me the can   sat & drew out his pipe

    "Keep it *msieu Birnee*
    you will feel more *en garde* at least
    These are the big Asians   *Blatta orientalis*
    most nimble   as you see   & (he lit his pipe)
    they wont take fire you know
    or choke in smoke   or drown"
An idea seemed to hit him   He eyed me solemnly
    "I could write perhaps the Gideon *compagnie*
    to bring me more Bibles

In time the digestion of these *cafards*
would be ruined by so much religion
However   meantime   those two
they shed their carapaces"
"—the devils!   (I broke in) & grow clean ones?"

"*D'accord* (Fred raised a crafty finger)
but they *eat* the old backs I sprayed"
He looked then so smug & *encyclopédique*
I had to needle him: "But dammit man
you cant go round wrenching drawers open all day
What about those you never see?" I got up
& pulled out all the others   Nothing
except   yes   that sewer smell

"*Ah!   les autres*" Fred murmured almost fondly
"Patience is necessary   acceptance even
There is a whole book about *les blattes*
You have read it perhaps? *Non*? (He puffed his pipe)
It says they were here 350,000,000 years ago
—some time before us it seems—
In the Carboniferous Age 800 species already
They are a good design   a model to last
like outriggers you might say   or pipes
Now there are 1200 species"
"What the hell's their secret, Fred?   Just toughness?"
"That yes (Fred was on his feet again
the lecturer at climax) but even more
they thrive on what the world has most to give
on shit   especially ours
& as you know   we double our production
every 50 years now"
"So how come they havent solved our sewage problems?"
"No doubt they will   but maybe solve us too
for they are most nur-tured it seems
by parthogens of polio they find in our debris
& as for germs of cholera & typhoid
it is possible they use them as aphrodisiacs or—
(just then Alua called him from the kitchen)—
at least as genetic stimulators
It must be coffee time   you will join us?"

Before I did I flipped open every drawer again
Of course nothing   except the stink, mephitic now
I took out all my gear & threw the airèsol
in the bottom drawer   & the Gideon after it
It may not happen in my lifetime I thought
as I closed the drawer firmly
but if humans survive another century
they'll have to land here fighting 10-foot Crotons
Christian roaches armoured for crusade
cucarachas high on lindichloridane as well as grass
& spraying distilled humanicide from every tentacle

Ovalau 1969

FOUR FEET BETWEEN

I was extending a patchwork of lint & batten
from ankle-sores to my new heel-cuts
absorbed in masochism & blessing my foresight
with bandaids   blessing too the voyagers
who brought breadfruit to Fiji
& this tree casting a benison of leaves
just where the volcano trail widens down
to the islet's only road
(though i'd conceded to myself
there were some million years of hindsight
before the breadfruit learned to grow
3-foot leaves & cannonball-sized seeds
to come to terms with perpetuity)
The cotton foliage on my purpling feet
argued however that i'd learned nothing much
from 60 years of being literate
nothing about coral poison anyway
or the agility of lava to mince mainland shoes

I was cosetting a raw big toe with my last band
when i grew conscious a slow pad of other feet
was on the trail   so close when i looked up
i caught myself in eyes deeplocked in a great face
Bula i said   trying to get it bass & guttural
His brows rose like wings   . *Bula bula*! he said
quickly & stepped back
I must have got my hello close
& waited now for that wide Melanesian grin of welcome
But his stare was pitchy & the long bones of his face
seemed set in suspicion   even hostility
I could read nothing of him nor guess his age
the skin rough leather but the blast of hair
sootblack as any youth's
My height & about twice my width he stood there
a dark tree of flesh on the basalt stones

Suddenly he spoke   but in Fijian
i fumbled out my 7 words to say i couldnt speak it
He went back to staring   & i to my toepatch
Rooster-crows had been filtering thru the mangroves
There must be a village close   & he from it
I tried to forget it was near here only 90 years ago
these natives ate their last missionary
A bulbul began bulbuling in the breadfruit overhead
It stopped & there was only the far surf breathing
& the two of us

Mis-e-ter   yalo vinaka   He groped for English
police a wat you name a?   E-ro-la i said *what's yours?*
He muttered something cave-deep & gruff
no way i could repeat it   Should i try standing
& shaking hands?   But now his arms flew wide
and gestured at the road   *You wait a for bussy?*
Toot toot?   His eyes went back to my feet
I told him i'd just been swimming in the crater falls
was returning to the guesthouse in the port
He dug some of that perhaps   but threw out a big chest
made swimstrokes & waved at the lagoon   *Wy you no?—*
Swim back by sea? i filled in   & tried
against a steady wrinkling of sepia forehead
to tell him i'd been snorkeling all week
just for the fun but got rolled on the coral
& the port doctor warned me off reefs
till the sores healed but then today i'd—
But he'd lost me near the start   Brows furrowed
like walnuts he bent over me   mouth muscles agonized
to find the right sounds   *Yeara   ow mucha yeara you?*
Sixty-five i said & fingered it   For the first time
he smiled   *Me!* he nodded his tall pompom
me too   sickyfi`!

That spark had leaped the wordgulf   We were egged on
I learned he'd even heard of Canada   *far side a Hawaii*
though he'd been born in the rooster's village
My lord i thought   he's only one generation
from Cannibal King Thakembau   I began pulling on my sox
& asked him if he'd been as far as Suva
His busby shook   *Sa sega   No alla tima here*
He looked more proud than sad
With a mahogany finger then he made an airy circle
You? You go rowna worela? Io i said *Yes*
& felt ashamed   He turned as if satisfied
but swung back & flung out at last the real question
E-ro-la   wat wrong a you feet?

I tried again & got nowhere   This wasnt tourist country
He'd never met a fullgrown man who went up the volcano
without a boar-spear   & swam in cold waterfalls
& dived in the sea only to be looking
But most of all he couldnt understand what hurt my feet
And so he stood   a statue of Melanic Power
maroon cheeks under a storm of hair
torso cicatriced with the darker scars of tribal rites
endured a half-century ago   a skirt of sorrel reeds
& all mounted on two unfeeling pedestals of meat
two tough sun-barbecued planksteaks of feet
like those his cousins use   across the bay on Benga
to walk on white-hot stones   for magic or for tourists

What's wrong my feet i said *is I not born here too*
He laughed   the only time   with a solid flash of teeth
Bussy come a some a time he said gently *you be o rite*
Ni sa mothe Goobye   He went paddling swiftly up the trail
You o-rite now i called   & lay back to wait the bus
under the breadfruit tree

Levuka 1969

1965-1974: Canada

WAY TO THE WEST

11 pm & sunset still going on
but that cd be the latitude
whats wrongs the colour
everywhere horseshit ochre & roiling
like paper that twists/browns
before firing up on hot ashes
theres somebodys hell ahead
meantime our lips prick
& the trees are dead

but it's another 20 miles before the sign
            You Are Entering
            S U D B U R Y
        Home of the world's largest
& christ there on the skull of a hill
3 manhattan-high stacks   a phallic calvary
ejaculating some essence of rotted semen
straight up like mass sabotage at cape kennedy

the damned are all over   the young
shrieking (looking much like anyone)
drag-race with radios up
from one smouldering stoplight to another—
under neon the older faces
assembled from half europe
screwcheeked/pitted all the same way
have something dignified about their devilship
that stares us down   till they come human
& houck brown on the cement

WELCOME TO . . .   73% OF THE FREE
       WORLD'S NICKEL IS CREATED HERE
& the free world invented a special cough
not even 100 taverns can dampen
nor all the jukes drown in the doorways
of pandemonium   milton thou shouldst
be living etc

DEAD END   wheres west?   sunset folded
our headlights finger dumped cans
wriggle through streets like crevasses
blasted in bedrock pink & folded
like glazed guts on a butchers marble

out of the starless dark falls the roar
of golgotha   how long before one stops
noticing?   & the sting in the eyes?

by a raped old car an indian sits
praying?   puking
             You Are Leaving
             S U D B U R Y
       Center of Free Enterprise
& 20 more miles of battlefield

at last a moon looms up
we are into the dumb firs again
       TURN OUT   300 YDS
             HISTORIC SITE
             FRENCH RIVER
what?   canoe route the Hurons found
& showed the whites—
the way to the west   silks   buffalo
vietnam   the moon
shines over the middle of nowhere—
dumb as the trees

we stop for a leak   silence
too late for other cars
the trees listen back
nothing   the owls dead too?

suddenly some kind of low growl
coming up!   we head back for the car—
only a night jet

but after it passes we realize
we'd been hearing the river all along

Northern Ontario 1965

IMAGEORGE & IMANGELA IN CALGARY

just being with you my patient friends
rolled all that gray gnurr up
that top inch flecked with craporatory
socred guano
veins of Old Dog pee
squirted down from prairie skies
into mashticks & luncheonshat

we scraped it off
rolled up the good white undersnow
got down to the sweet grass again

ive brought some snow back
made a Snowmagog & Snowmangela
they stand unmelting on my slumsunporch

Snowmagog is taller
he has angles
his arms are really baseball bats
agate alleys are his eyes
set in sockets oblong
like Tlaloc
for he is a raingog
showering poems everywhere

Snowmangela has curves
& is snowmangelic
reflects all sunshifts
warms my old porch
while Snowmageorge he plays it cool
sends imagoes daynightly flashing

i put this wordscreen round them
in hope to scare off dogs a little while
oldeastern gritshit in smogonto
keep snoot from them
from you
so hold you shining
totemagically

Toronto 1965

MEN'S SPORTSWEAR DEPT

looking beyond the head
of the squatting clerk
bald as a mushroom
while he hunts me out
an ankle support
i see there's a nasty dry wound
in the back of one pink calf
of every dummy in tennis shorts
vibrant on pedestals around us
up which disappears
an iron bar
(also riveted to the floor)

is it to prevent
those brightcheeked lads
from being goosed
by some gay shopper?
or even ravaged
quite away?

no   now that i turn
to the non-dummies
(passing & in the mirror)
i see these curled immortals
are impaled only to prevent them
from shuddering
when brushed against

Montréal 1965

IN PURDY'S AMELIASBURG
(first visit, 1965)

But Al   this round pond man—
        where's Roblin Lake   I mean the real one?
        where's that great omphalos I know
        corpsegray below apocalyptic skies?
    this cosy girl's-belly-button
    brims with rosewater
    from one of those frilly May sunsets

Dont get me wrong   I'm grateful to be here
    after Toronto
        still hairy from a long winter
    after Trenton
        that raped that hustled town
it's good here it's peace the blackbirds
are setting off their own springs in the air
    but the air's too bright
it could be I've come the wrong time
    too soon for those horsecrap-fattened peonies
    you reddened the shores with
    too late for skulldeep snow
    stubborn in the fence zags
man there's only dandelions
barring the way to the privy

But no what's wrong is place as well
it's anybody's church across the lake
    the spire shrank
    and that carpenter who fixed it once
    against the sky is off in Trenton
    banging thumbnails and wallboard
    is you in fact
and you're not here   your mouse is hiding
quote representative of an equally powerful race unquote
that heron   the cosmic crying rays
    where in Roblin are they?

In this Ameliasburg a backyard of stones
is where they trucked off Roblin Mill
        declared historical enough
        for reassembly in Toronto
by god they'll whisk your own shack away
if you dont stop writing
        (and Eurithe too the ferocious wife)
        and the very cowpads before your eyes

Al I think they have
I think Somebody's cleaned up
        after your picknicking glaciers
they've raised the roof on the shack
        ringed it with Summer Homes
        told Ptolemy to leave town
        made your spouse patient and young again
it's the Same People of course
        who took the wolves away
        from Malcolm Lowry's woods
        sent Eliot's London Bridge to Arizona
        smoothed Jeffers' headlands back
        into Californian hills
so though it's fine here of course
        it's not Ameliasburg

But wait
        what's popping up when I sweep the kitchen?
                half an envelope
                with half a poem scribbled
and from behind the battered wood-heater
        yet another empty bottle
        smelling absolutely of wild grape

Next morning I drift down a nebulous way
             to the village hardware
             like a madman's tiny museum
             Can-opener   yep   got one
             got one all right   You in a hurry?
             yeah   got mislaid some time back
             I'd have to look   drop in nex week mebbe

I return under the ancient clouds
      the Lake is hazy   endless
what bird is flapping away?
the shack's doorknob turns planetary in my hand—
      Al that's your mouse on the floor bowing!

FOUND SWAHILI SERENADE / A JUKOLLAGE

this is my song
        (petula clark)
i got a feeling
until you love someone
every little bit hurts

hey darling
i'm a man
        (englebert humperdinck)
i cant get enough of it
till it's time for you to go

the river is wide
going down for the third time
i will not cry
sad story

Yonge Street, Toronto 1965

GIOVANNI CABOTO / JOHN CABOT

fourteen hundred and ninety seven
giovanni sailed from the coast of devon

    52 days   discovered cape breton n.s.
    or maybe cape race (or labrador?)

    caught some cod
    went back to england
    with 16 bear hides
    (none prime)

    told henry 7
    his majesty now owned
    cipango   land of jewels
    "abounding moreoever in silks
    & brasilwode"
    also the spice islands of asia
    and the country of the grand khan

    henry gave giovanni 30 quid
    to go back to nova scotia

who was kidding who?

Chestnut Park Road 1965

POET-TREE 1

POET-TREE 2

i fear that i shall never make
a poem slippier than a snake
or oozing with as fine a juice
as runs in girls or even spruce
no i wont make not now nor later
pnomes as luverlee as pertaters
trees is made by fauns or satyrs
but only taters make pertaters
& trees is grown by sun from sod
& so are the sods who need a god
but poettrees lack any clue
they just need me   & maybe you

Savary Island, B.C. 1950/Scarborough College 1966

HOKKAI IN THE DEW LINE SNOWS

to sleep under real
stars   wake in the pupil of
original Sun

goodmornings with birds
love naked by waterfalls
o best planet—   whoooM!

a north door opens
the leaves scurry to hole &
the Cat prowls our world

Trumansburg, N.Y. 1966

PEI

O here is an isle
where the sands run for miles
but the lobster's not here for the plucking
the water's berg cold
& the ladies are told
that only Milt Acorn says fucking

Cabot Strait 1966

OUR FOREFATHERS LITERARY

our forefathers literary
had little laugh or quippery
even Can.Lit. profs are uncertain
about Haliburton
and all their students reassembling
Carman's skeleton
never found the funny bone
(beware the jokes of Archibald Lampman
they'll give you cramp man)
Grove was grave and Mair still more
and though they made a Baron out of Parker
his prose just went on getting darker
Sir Charles G. D. Roberts couldnt see
in all his g.d. woods, Silenus in a tree

well yes there was our northern loon our Leacock
subtle as a duck   and laughing like a peacock

Fredericton, N.B. 1966

NEWFOUNDLAND
(for E. J. Pratt)

n **e** w f o u n **d** l a n d
n e w **f o u n d** l a n d
n **e** **w** f o u n d **l a n d**
n e w f **o** u **n** d l a n d
n e w f o u n d **l** a n **d**
n e w **f o** u n d **l** a n **d**
n e w f o u n d **l a n d**
n e **w** f o u n d l **a n** d
n e **w** f o u n d **l** a n **d**
n e w **f o u n d** l a n d
n **e** w f o u n d **l a n** d
n e w f o u n d **l a n d**
n e w **f o u n** d l a n d
n e w **f o u n** d l a **n d**
n e **w** f o u n d l **a n** d
n e w f o **u** n d l a n d
n **e** w f o u n d l a **n d**

St. John's, Newfoundland

MESSYJESTS FOR A KINAGEING KITCHMESS

1. kitchmess day cure-all

> God rust ye merry gintilemen
> Let nuthin you dizzmay
> Tamorrah Armafuckingeddon comes
> but not on Kitchmess Day

Rev yer moters
salt the snow
burn the octane high
smash the bawtls
cut the trees
an let the missuls fly

Like Christ brawt Luvn Peace taday
ree-lax man its gif—
the Bomb aint doo till Bawxn Day
—is still the twenny-fitt

2. *wuz eight nights before kitchmess*

wuz eight nights before kitchmess
enawl throo Eatsomes n Symptoms
evry creature wuz buyen reeturnbul gif coupons
Legfulls uv pantyhose pranced on th counters
coz th chimneys wur gawn
butta plastic Sane Nick wuz lid up on eej lawn
Th kids wur all nestled with speed by thur tellies
while visions uv spacewar currdeld thur bellies
an mom inner peasant skirt en noo fun fur over
wuz checkn th sitter ta see wuz she sober
Th moon onna breast uv th noo-faln snow
wuz a highriser spotlight thut wispert *Ho Ho*!
(HO HO. . . . .Ho Ho. . . . .Ho ho. . . . . .ho ho. . . . . . .ho)
wen wot ta my wunnerin gaze didda peer
butta cracked flyn sawsur with enflateabul deer
anna two-heddit Sanna who said widda leer
"A beriberi Kitchmesss anna Grippy Dew Near!"

Massey College 1966/1973

Good year for movie **nuns**

trying to break into the Canadian souvenir market with Expo '67 in sight. For this they have sealskin hats

FRIARS A Go Go
Where the Action is

Estee Lauder's Re-Nutriv lipstick in amber glow, peach glow or petal glow. 3.75. Refills 2.75.

$2,000 down, $19,500 and up, all brick. Solid brick detached 6 and 7-room bungalows. Attached garages, stone front.

For Unattached people only — 21 OR OVER

organ, etc.) have a true baroque tone that will make your ears tingle. SOUND: Lovingly done.

Eskimo now living has ever seen a Toonik.

Predicts Indian race riots

But many a silent tear is shed While others are asleep.

BLADDER IRRITATION MAY DISTURB SLEEP

"The U.S. is finding that water is one of its most valuable and becoming one of its scarcest resources, and we have, well, we have lots of water."

Mr. Pearson said the U.S. is "anxious to work out arangements by which some of our water resources are moved down south.

"This could be one of the most important developments in our history," Mr. Pearson said.

cient. Bikinis are accessible on every beach there are 3,600 miles of beaches), but women dressy in the cities and a lady will feel conspicuous in slacks or shorts.

to about 50 people attended a three-day teach-in sponsored by the Iroquois at the Royal York Hotel. It is an attempt to make their grievances known.

"All of us want peace. But asking for the withdrawal of ....eans will not bring peace. It would be so easy to take

Every day in some small way Memories of you come our way.

For Exciting Lip Radiance

He warned that some day Kenora, Sault Ste. Marie and North Battleford will be new Los Angeles.

Virgo. Special word to Aquarius: Be considerate of favors by those who perform special services.

THE GREATEST STORY EVER TOLD

Hats of famous on sale in Ottawa

OTTAWA (CP) — Hats that have graced famous female's heads will be sold at an Ottawa charity bazaar today.

The wives of Governor-General George Vanier, Prime Minister Lester Pearson, and Opposition leader John Diefenbaker have contributed bonnets, along with a woman senator and Charlotte Whitton, former mayor of Ottawa.

STONE CHURCH

45 DAVENPORT ROAD, WA. 1-7939 ALBERT G. VATERS, Pastor

9.45 — CHRISTIAN EDUCATION HOUR

Speaker: PASTOR VATERS

11 A.M.

"LET'S USE FORCE"

7 P.M.

"THIS GOSPEL OF CHRIST"

TUES. 8 P.M. BIBLE STUDY   FRI. 8 P.M. FAMILY NIGHT

SO YOU HAVE THE FEELING I HAVE -- THAT WE'VE KNOWN EACH OTHER SOME PLACE BEFORE?

An agnostic who preaches at Willowdale Unitarian Fellowship says he is getting "a good response" from children to his Sunday School course that claims Christ was insane.

Here are 12 love songs, with a big, bouncy sound. Ray Conniff drives his orchestra and singer

NOT A CO-OP
But not Inook Ltd. It is a company and not a co-op.

and there are clips of more than 40 love goddesses of the last 50 years. They

A Quebec separatist last night recommended a Cuba-style revolution for his province—meaning, don't tell the truth until you've won.

Professor Jacques Lucques of the University of Montreal said, "we are for complete independence and socialism."

But he added that "a lot of people in Quebec are allergic to the words communism and socialism" and "we have got to take into consideration that Uncle Sam is not far from here. If we win the revolution tomorrow and lose it the next day, it is no good."

Separatist wants Cuba-style

Toronto 1967

I ACCUSE US
(speech, anti-vietnam rally, toronto, 1967)

O.K. so the u.s. is the only country
to move "from barbarism to decadence
without achieving civilization"
& where does that leave us?
what's with us supernorthamericans
who never had the guts
to be either barbaric or decadent?
are we what the Yanks have fostered
instead of a civilization?

Hail!   five hundred years
of near-beer British
& sour-wine French
united in building Unamerica
without speaking to each other
(also farewell!   twenty thousand years
of Indian & Inuit
& the creatures they lived with)

Sure we're into our second century
of well-not-quite parasitism
& not-quite-independence
Hail!   fellow-hitchhikers
in the limousines of empires
It's been fast smooth riding
but where are we heading?
If we have to be fleas
leaving a dead lion
why choose a sick eagle?
Why not a healthy sheep?
or really live it big:
think rape & hunt for elephants?

Sorry   I forgot   we are Canadians
we are the quiet reasoning folk
the blessed peacemakers in fact
who shall inherit
the radioactive earth
Balls!   as neutrals
we're about as phony as they come
We are the experts in waging
neither-war-nor-peace
while making up our Canamind

We are the boys who put delegates
on the United Nations' commission
to keep real peace in Vietnam
& secretly told them
not to report the shiploads of arms
the U.S. unloaded weekly in Saigon

We are the owners of the biggest swatch
of "undeveloped resources" in the world
(i.e. uncut trees ungouged earth
unkilled fish unscalped animals
unoiled beaches & unblasted rock)
all of which we are hot to unpossess
if only our capital werent tied up
making more explosives to export
for wars abroad than we use at home
for our kind of peace

Yes sir we're the biggest seller
of napalm & phosphorus
the U.S. ever had
though of course we howl
every week on television
when the bastards drop it all
on somebody's kids

Don't think we haven't got a conscience—
who sent a whole children's hospital
to South Vietnam?   O sorry no
that was the British   Our doctors
werent allowed to sew new eyelids & skin
on little gooks that got in the road
of free enterprise by c.i.l. (Canada)

For Christ's or Buddha's sake or for our Own
let's face us as others do
Even the Americans who've escaped to us
from the earth's most prosperous
& brutal superstate
the unartful dodgers mistaking
our inaction for bravery
& our ambiguities for freedom
find our uniqueness lies
in "dynamic apathy"

Hell Vietnam was just a symptom
we've got the disease!
When the Greek army's fascists
murdered Greek democracy
who at once assured the generals
they'd get a loan?
Yep that was Canada my fellow Ca-nadas
that was the frecklecheeked kid sister
beating Big Brother to it

Tomorrow it'll be our turn
to help somebody else
help kill more Jews Arabs
Polynesians whathaveyou
or sit firm in words for both sides
while the real Africans stand up
to be shredded down

It's us I accuse   you   me
of failure to become something else
than a dozen separatisms
united only by a common war
on our own central government
& by common exploitation
of our poor by our rich

I accuse us
of failure to become a nation—
a nation neither White Red Black Brown or Pink
but its own Rainbow
a nation seeking internationhood
not another empire   a Soul
a Human Presence   capable of pity with strength
of less holiness   & more wholeness

I accuse Us
of celebrations without cause
of standing not moving
in passionate urgency
towards the *real* civilization
there may just be time
to glimpse before our species
crawls off to join the dinosaurs.

CHARITÉ, ESPÉRANCE ET FOI
(a tender tale from early ca-nada)

Once there were 3 little Indian girls
Champlain adopted them from the Montagnais
to show King Louis & the Cardinal it was possible
to make Christian Ladies out of savages
He baptized them Foi (11) Espérance (12) et Charité (15)
then put them in a fort to learn their French

Little Faith wriggled away & split for the woods
but Hope & Charity quickly mastered irregular verbs
& sewing   developed bosoms   went on to embroidery
When Champlain saw they had acquired piety & table manners
he dressed them in style & sailed downstream to Tadoussac
en route to the French Court with Espérance et Charité

But a wicked merchant named Nicholas Marsolet of Tadoussac
got Espérance aside & told her she was what he had to have
She said she had a date in France with King & God
Nick snarled he could have her & her sister given back
to the Indians   & grabbed her round her corset
She pulled a knife & got away to Charité

Les deux étudiantes then wrote Nicholas a letter
Hope began it:
    "Monsieur Marsolet, it was an honour & a pleasure to
    meet you, & I look forward to our next rencontre.
    In anticipation I have sharpened my knife so that
    I may on that occasion give myself the added joy
    of cutting out your heart"
& Charity added:
    "It will give me, monsieur, great pleasure
    to help my sister eat it."
All this sounded more elegant in the original of course
because that was in correct seventeenth-century French

They showed their letter to Champlain
He was impressed   no mistakes in tenses
He told them he was proud they had stood firm
especially against that méchant marchand Marsolet
who ate meat both Fridays & Saturdays   an Anglophile
& sold hooch to their cousin Indians in Tadoussac
However   Champlain added   he didnt think
that Espérance et Charité were ready yet for France

The two young ladies wept   unrolled their broderie
Champlain agreed they were bien civilisées
They went down on their knees   showed him their petticoats
Champlain was kind   admired the sewing   but was firm
It was France   he said   that wasnt ready yet for them
He gave them each a wooden rosary
& sent them back to Québec with Guillaume Couillard

Couillard was a respectable churchwarden & crop inspector
no merchant   he couldnt read & had 10 children of his own
He was the first to use the plough in Canada

but when Champlain got back from France nobody knew
where Hope & Charity had got to
or if they ever found their Faith again

Montréal 1967

1984 MINUS 17 & COUNTING AT
U OF WATERLOO ONTARIO

after the calorestimated meal
in the male hall
they walk back to the compulibratories
keeping to the asphalt paths
conceived by the landtects

sometimes a thousand are in forward motion
engimechs the plureality   at 0826 hrs
in pairs   with crewcuts   hands by flanks
& slightly crooked below rainbreakers (yellow)
with *U of W* on back
ENGINEERS on upper sleeve L
& black number upper R

since none of this is actually required by deans
nor the gloves (black)   hushpuppies (gray)
nor absence of headcover & expression
what is felt is communiternity   a campustalt

the mathamen   cruts not quite so short
are sometimes grouped in 3s
but otherwise all waterloobed:
hands by flanks & slightly . . . (yellow) . . .
MATHS on . . . black . . . gray . . . absence
almost as striking—communalove at least

a few artsies yet (terminal class of '71)
midearburns / 1 in 10
dress as above of course
but some have briefcases in R hand
wear their ARTS upon their sleeves
& walk alone

1967

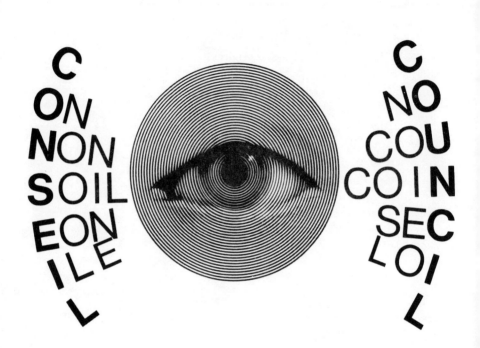

CANADA COUNCIL

Ottawa 1967

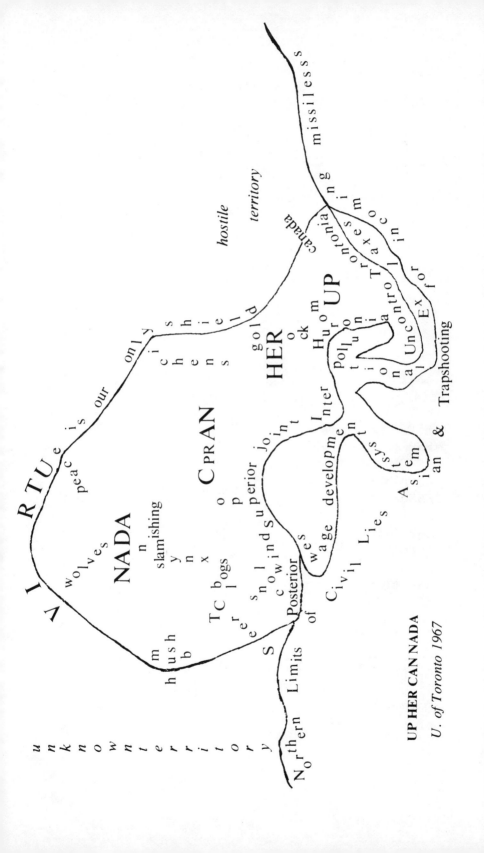

UP HER CAN NADA
U. of Toronto 1967

```
U N I V E R S I T Y
U N I V E R S E D
U N V E R S E D
U N S E R V E
U N E V E R
U N I T E
U N E W
U N O
U N
U
```

Guelph, Ontario 1967

ESTHER

ESPECTACULAR
ESPONTANEA
*ES*PORADICA
*ES*PARCIDA
*ES*SENTIAL
*ES*TRELLA
*ES*PUELA
ESPOSA
*ES*SER
*ES*PUMOSA
*ES*PERANDA
*ES*TUPENDA
*ES*TRUENDOSA
*ES*TIMULANTE
ESTRAMBOTICA

Rosedale 1967

CXAT bilingual

North Bay, Ontario 1967

WINDOW SEAT

40 ft of wing out there
suddenly i want to walk
into that sun
but capt loudspeaker says
headwinds 105 mph speed another 400
at once im walking back on air

!BUT WHAT A FUN DEATH!

                                    alt 35000
                            nothing but
                    7
            miles of
high dive
at last i can practice   k
    g   c   n
  a   a   i
      i   j   f
r s   n   e
      e   s

                            o   a   r
                        b   d
s   p   r   i   n   g   i
                                           n
d o w n   g
        from   c l o u d
                            to   c l o u d

(o yes acceleration 32 ft per sec per sec)
but ive 7 m to play with
& all that wind d r i f t
  & b o d yf l a p t

ive got time at last to break the world
's record for b (i once dreamed about) s^om

<pre>
        a   e
        c   r
        k   s
                           a l
                            u t
                             s
</pre>

before straightening into a

<pre>
        AA
        SS
        WW
  N   N AA   N N
     N N NN N   N
           ∀
</pre>

so widearmed & precise i am

<pre>
                 e
embracing s e   !
             e
               e
</pre>

the whole world & time
in one last sweet tick of li—

but no one lets me walk out
too hard to break this doubleglass
i'll have to be content again
with the usual smooth landing
dead on
& the meek shuffle into the pens
to wait my turn somewhere
at ground level
under the overcast ahead.

Edmonton, Alberta 1969

FOR MY WIFE

o what can i do for my little gray mare
& what must she do with me?

i'm hardly a horse at all any more
a wrinkled bonebag is all
& she—she's a trotter & kicks her small legs
over the fence & into new grass

when i'm in the paddock & ass to the wind
prancing she comes & bites me out
to run in the sun with the fillies
& she whinnies ahead like a foal

o how can i keep with my nipping gray mare
& how can she wait for me?

Vancouver 1969

<table>
<tr><td colspan="3" align="center">1977   # COLANDER   1977
(with monkly potes & a pnome*)</td></tr>
</table>

JANISSARY	CASSIWARY	MARSH
1 2 3 4 5 6 7 8 9 10 11 12 13 14 15 16 17 18 19 20 21 22 23 24 25 26 27 28 29 30 31	1 2 3 4 5 6 7 8 9 10 11 12 13 14 15 16 17 18 19 20 21 22 23 24 25 26 27 28	1 2 3 4 5 6 7 8 9 10 11 12 13 14 15 16 17 18 19 20 21 22 23 24 25 26 27 28 29 30 31
eloi ogg	mai chin chu	abe rillway
RAPERY	**MAJOR**	**JUBILEE**
1 2 3 4 5 6 7 8 9 10 11 12 13 14 15 16 17 18 19 20 21 22 23 24 25 26 27 28 29 30	1 2 3 4 5 6 7 8 9 10 11 12 13 14 15 16 17 18 19 20 21 22 23 24 25 26 27 28 29 30 31	1 2 3 4 5 6 7 8 9 10 11 12 13 14 15 16 17 18 19 20 21 22 23 24 25 26 27 28 29 30
jan s waring	fred v waring	marcia prill
OPPOSIGHT	**AMBER**	**HOGTOE**
1 2 3 4 5 6 7 8 9 10 11 12 13 14 15 16 17 18 19 20 21 22 23 24 25 26 27 28 29 30 31	1 2 3 4 5 6 7 8 9 10 11 12 13 14 15 16 17 18 19 20 21 22 23 24 25 26 27 28 29 30 31	1 2 3 4 5 6 7 8 9 10 11 12 13 14 15 16 17 18 19 20 21 22 23 24 25 26 27 28 29 30
d c m burr	toby gnome	bernault femmebeurre
BURNOFF	**EMBER**	**SOMBRE**
1 2 3 4 5 6 7 8 9 10 11 12 13 14 15 16 17 18 19 20 21 22 23 24 25 26 27 28 29 30 31	1 2 3 4 5 6 7 8 9 10 11 12 13 14 15 16 17 18 19 20 21 22 23 24 25 26 27 28 29 30	1 2 3 4 5 6 7 8 9 10 11 12 13 14 15 16 17 18 19 20 21 22 23 24 25 26 27 28 29 30 31
m burgeon	jeanne ouaire	ossip m birrock

* Pnomes are gnomic mnemonic pomes to dismember things like the kooks of the monk and who wrode them.

PNOME

Thirdy days hath Rapery
Ember, Hogtoe, Jubilee,
All the rest have thirdy-one
Except Cassiwary the dumb
Which never gets the countdown right
from Amber through to Opposight

TORONTO MARCH

7.59 a.m.
& now this message

(despite the white flak
descending
on the black ruins
of barricades &
whirling the tires
to screams of impotence
i know
the revolution is flowering
somewhere

or how could they be hauling
captives
into the markets of paris
this moment battalions
of defiant muguet
sold in the streets

& yesterday the reports were
vancouver infiltrated
even in halifax
someday the rebels

let's keep our pistils taut
powder dry
buds will explode
scent will be used
see the young coming
to save the world)

8.00 a.m.
here is the news
in south-east asia bombers . . .
an explosion in montréal has . . .
riots again last night   in . . .
toronto's air pollution index . . .
tomorrow noon is the deadline for . . .
(i'd forgotten
it's only a vegetable revolution
once again)

& now to summarise
the news is *it could be*
the last . . .
8.02 a.m.
& now this mes—

Isabella Street 1970

FIRST FLIGHT

Before i was 5 i knew
i was different   a bird   at least
if only left alone
in the right place
ide fly
the polegate to th corral wd do
was out of kitchenwindow sight
     my mom
     cd watch me later
     from th ground
i said a Gentle Jesus
more to warn him i was comin up
than fear i wdnt
& took off
arms flappin from th highest bar

th trouble was
    (i realized
    just before i started howlin)
somebody was watchin
all along
    th hogs

later ive made my takeoffs
strictly without blabs
to Those Above

but damned if ever ive got set
on th top rail of any gate
without i hear a rooster crow
    & sense a row of snouts
    between th pigpen slats

Utica, N.Y. 1970

ANCIENT CANABARDIC LAMENT

it's the whole wild world
i want to make
but the bitch still says *mañana*
wont even wait
while i masturbate
more *canadiana*

Washington, D.C. 1970

FOUND PAEAN TO VANCOUVER
BY RUDYARD KIPLING (1890)*

A great sleepiness
lies on Vancouver
as compared with an American town:
men don't fly
up and down streets
telling lies
and the spittoons
in the delightfully comfortable hotel
are unused;
the baths are free
and their doors are unlocked. . . .
I thank God for it.
Give me hewn granite . . . and peace. . . .
All that Vancouver wants
is a fat earthwork fort
upon a hill—
there are plenty of hills—
a selection of big guns,
a couple of regiments of infantry,
and later a big arsenal. . . .
It is not seemly
to leave unprotected
the head-end
of a big railway;
for though Victoria and Esquimalt,
our naval stations, . . . are very near,
so also is . . . Vladivostock.

*(*From Sea to Sea*, ch. xxviii; *Complete Works*, Doubleday, vol. 18, pp. 46-47)

LooN about to laugh

England 1944/Vancouver 1970

Tsawassen 1970

DAYBREAK ON LAKE OPAL: HIGH ROCKIES

as
the
fire
from
opals
a trem
-ulous
dawn be-
gins its
ceremony of
s l o w touch
without palms
its breath with-
out breathing along
the whorled turrets
moving shimmering fall
-ing over the scarred for
-ever-by-the-wind-besieged
ramparts the icecracked tree-
breached walls   the light of
the untouchable Sun sliding from
skyblue into the chill broken flesh
of our lifedrop   warming freeing the
silence of jays and firtops   sending a
heather of wind over unfolding asters and
eaglets   ruffling the moated lake to a green
soul and rolling once more the upraised sacrifice
of our world into the sword of Its P R E S E N C E

1946/1970

ON THE NIGHT JET

small waffle-irons glowing
on a huge farmhouse stove
crossroad towns of the prairies
seven miles below

faint rods of highways
electroscopic genes

mainly only the stars
of the farms
lonely as the others
like reflections above
(below?)
and as remote
from me
now
on the night
jet

Over Saskatchewan 1970

ALPHABIRNEY

Toronto 1973

CANADA: CASE HISTORY: 1973

No more the highschool land
deadset in loutishness
This cat's turned cool
the gangling's gone
guffaws are for the peasants

Inside his plastic igloo now
he watches gooks and yankees bleed
in colour on the telly
But under a faded Carnaby shirt
ulcers knife the rounding belly

Hung up on rye and nicotine and sex-
y flicks, kept off the snow and grass
he teeters tiptoe on his arctic roof
(ten brittle legs, no two together)
baring his royal canadian ass
white and helpless in the global winds

Schizoid from birth, and still a sado-masochist
this turkey thinks that for his sins
he should be carved while still alive:
legs to Québec, the future Vietnam;
the rest, self-served and pre-digested,
to make a Harvest Home for Uncle Sam. . . .

Teeth shot and memory going
(except for childhood grudges),
one moment murderous, the next depressed,
this youth, we fear, has moved from adolescence
into what looks like permanent senescence.

Toronto 1973

BESTIARY

an arkfull she is
of undulant creatures
a cinamon bearcub
curled in a warm ball
thinking of honey & berries
nuts roots or even
grass jelly for supper

a sturdy racoon too
with masked eyes
& dexterous forepaws
very frequent to bathe
& a bandit of ice cream
who sleeps a lot
with one soft hindpaw
poking most modestly out

or a shy bobcat
coloured olivebrown
or maybe pale gold
with round
slipper-fur feet
on which she sits very quiet
and so thoughtful
beside her leafy plants
she is sometimes invisible
though very much there

she can be an ochre
squirrel as well
sinuous & all compact
alert & frisky
& away & back like a dream

& whatever creature
she is its peaceful emissary
most faithful
& most loving

Toronto 1974

NO BODY

i walk home in snow-slush
plodding alone imagining
the leap of pulse
under your graywool glove

snow slants down
an endless flock
of tiny bird-flakes
over me they wheel
and for a while move upward
having nowhere to fall
since you went away

the flat's not real
like a room "restored"
in a Pioneer Museum
exact but unconvincing
where is the being
who gave the armchair meaning?
i do not think
the TV will turn on

your small slippers
wait by the chesterfield
they do not move
something arranged
by a slick director
they lack the feet
which are human and complete
with miniscule callouses

i water the yellow chrysanthemum
silent as a photograph
nothing drinks or stirs

only the bed grows
and is heard
it is twice as big already
and noisily empty
and yet an imitation too
a stuffed animal
nothing warm under the fur
or soft
no
body

Alexander Street, Toronto 1973

SHE IS
(for wailan, on her 24th birthday)

she is
fresh every way
herself
like a dawn

when warm winds come
she will move
all her body
in a tremble of light

but today she stands
in magical stillness
she has clasped
all my falling flakes
from the round of her sky
and wished them
into her own
snowtree

through the cold time
she holds me
with evergreen
devotion
she bears up my whiteness

o so light may i press
letting each needle
grow in her own
symmetry

for i am at peace
in her form
after whirling
and faithful to all
her curves

but when warm winds come
we must stir from this trance
she will lift living arms
to the sun's dance

i will slide then
in a soft caress
of her brown sides
and my falling will end
somewhere in her roots

may my waters then
bring her strength only
help her hold trim
and evergreen her being
with suns and winds
for o many and many
and happiest years

Treehouse, Uxbridge 1974

INDEX OF TITLES

Earle Birney

Earle Birney was born in Calgary, Alberta, in 1904. He was educated at the Universities of British Columbia, Toronto, California and London. In 1936 he was appointed lecturer in English at the University of Toronto, after having taught at the Universities of Utah and British Columbia. From 1936-40 he was literary editor of *The Canadian Forum*. He served as a personnel officer overseas during World War II. In 1945 he joined the International Shortwave Service of the C.B.C. From 1946 to 1963 he was professor of English at the University of British Columbia, and of creative writing from 1963-65. He won Governor-General's Awards for poetry in 1942 and 1945 and the Leacock Medal for Humour in 1949. In 1952 he received the Lorne Pierce Medal for Literature from the Royal Society of Canada. He was awarded the Canada Council Medal ''for outstanding cultural achievement'' in 1968. Earle Birney has been writer-in-residence at the Universities of Toronto and Waterloo, and Regents Professor at the University of California.

An extensive world traveller, Mr. Birney has read his poetry to audiences across Canada and in many foreign lands. Selections of his poems have been published in Britain and the United States. At present, he is on a world tour, reading his poetry and working on other books.